Exchange 2010

A Practical Approach

By Jaap Wesselius

D1438417

First published by Red Gate Books 2009

Copyright Jaap Wesselius 2009

ISBN 978-1-906434-32-8

Technical Review by Michael B Smith

Cover Image by Paul Vlaar

Edited by Chris Massey

Typeset & Designed by Matthew Tye & Gower Associates

Copy Edited by Una Campbell

Table of Contents

About the Author

Jaap Wesselius is the founder of DM Consultants, a company with a strong focus on Messaging and Collaboration solutions. Together with three co-workers, he works 24 x 7 on Exchange Server solutions. In fact, he's being doing that ever since Exchange Server 4.0 came out, long, long ago in 1995.

After working in Microsoft for eight years, Jaap decided, in 2006, that the time had come to leave Redmond and start his own business. This was also the period when he got a chance to commit more of his time to the Exchange community in The Netherlands, resulting in an Exchange Server MVP award in 2007 that he's held ever since. Jaap is also a regular contributor at the Dutch Unified Communications User Group (HTTP://WWW.UCUG.NL), and a regular author for Simple-Talk (HTTP://WWW.SIMPLE-TALK.COM). Besides Exchange Server, Jaap really likes to work with Hyper-V and, as a result, also founded the Dutch Hyper-V community in early 2008.

When time permits (and it never permits enough), Jaap savors life with his wife and three sons, and also enjoys doing some serious hiking and cycling when he gets the chance. It's an ongoing dream of his to hike or cycle across Europe, but this will probably always stay a dream for as long as he spends his time writing.

About the Technical Reviewer

Michael B. Smith is an Exchange MVP who owns and operates a consulting firm that specializes in Exchange Server and Active Directory. He has over 25 years of experience in the IT field, and focuses on providing solutions that support customers' goals for operational excellence. Michael is also a well-known writer for such publications as WindowsITPro, Exchange Messaging & Outlook, to name just two. He also recently completed his second book, *"Monitoring Exchange Server 2007 with Operations Manager,"* and was technical editor for two other books, recently published with O'Reilly Media: *"Active Directory, Fourth Edition"* and *"Active Directory Cookbook, Third Edition."* Michael is active in a number of online Exchange communities, and you can read his blog at:

HTTP://THEESSENTIALEXCHANGE.COM/BLOGS/MICHAEL

Acknowledgements

This is my first book, and I wasn't actually planning to write one. I tried to write a book on Exchange Server Disaster Recovery in the past, but Exchange Server changes so significantly with each Service Pack that I ended up rewriting quite a lot of my material every six months. After realizing this was a never-ending story, I made a tactical decision to quit while I was ahead...

...until early 2009, when Michael Francis asked me if I'd ever considered writing a book. He persuaded me to try again, and I'm really thankful to him. Also Michael B. Smith as my Technical Reviewer, Steven van Houttum as a local Dutch peer, everybody from the Red Gate team and the people from the Exchange Server MVP Group – you were all very helpful. Thank you all.

I guess my wife and sons suffered the most when I was behind my laptop, writing again, and trying to figure out what was going wrong "*this time.*" The legacy of beta software, I'm afraid. And when things got really annoying, I went out hiking or cycling to clear my mind. Oh boy, isn't it lovely to write a book? :-)

And to anybody else, especially in my local community (who really don't know anything about Exchange Server, but know a lot about potatoes, onions, cows and stuff...), this is my book. And I have to be honest, it's not about "love at first sight" as I've said for such a long time... Maybe one day I'll write a novel, but right now I stick to technical books. I hope you like it, and I'd love to know what you think of it. Feel free to send me a note at

MYBOOK@JAAPWESSELIUS.NL.

Cheers,

Jaap Wesselius

Introduction

Being a trainer, I always wonder why official curriculums are so theoretical and lack so many real-world scenarios, which would surely be the most useful thing to learn about. In my articles for Simple-Talk, I *always* try to write about real-world scenarios and that's also the case for this book, hence *"A Practical Guide."*

Of course, you need some theory as well. Without knowing anything about Active Directory you'll never understand what Exchange Server 2010 is doing and why things are the way they are. But I tried to write all chapters from an administrator's perspective – what steps you have to take, and why. It's nothing like an Exchange Server 2010 Resource Kit, it's more a practical approach, hence the title of the book.

I wrote five chapters, covering the following topics.

Chapter 1 is an overall chapter – what's new in Exchange Server 2010 and what has deprecated with respect to Exchange Server 2007. Also there's some information regarding Active Directory, the three containers in Active Directory and some information regarding Active Directory sites.

Chapter 2 is an installation chapter dealing with a fresh installation of Exchange Server 2010 and the subsequent basic configuration to get it up and running.

Chapter 3 is the coexistence chapter and it probably deals with most scenarios; installing Exchange Server 2010 in an existing Exchange Server 2003 or Exchange Server 2007 environment.

Chapter 4 is about managing the Exchange environment using the Exchange Management Console, the Exchange Management Shell and the Exchange Control Panel. And, real cool in Exchange Server 2010, are the remote options in PowerShell version 2.

Chapter 5 is the high availability chapter. It deals with the new continuous replication when using Database Availability Groups, the best Exchange Server high availability solution ever made.

I realize I have not, and cannot, cover all aspects of Exchange Server 2010 in five chapters. Just for a start, think about the Unified Messaging role for integration with your telephony system, or integration with Office Communication Server (OCS) R2 for presence information and Instant Messaging. These are significant topics in their own right, and will make good chapters for an R2 or SP1 release of the book! There are a lot of areas I just can't cover here (even though I want to), and a lot more depth I could go into but, because I wanted to make this a light, quick-start book and not an Exchange Server 2010 "Bible," I've had to be very focused. I hope you find that focus useful, and this guide practical.

Summarizing Exchange Server 2010 – A practical approach

Given that this book was supposed to be a *practical approach* to Exchange Server 2010, I've tried to guide you through the new platform without writing a complete Resource Kit – I'll leave that to Microsoft. There's not a lot I can add at this stage but, in case you need some sound bites (maybe to convince your manager to let you upgrade), I'll give one last, lightning-quick round-up of what's new in Exchange Server 2010:

- By far the most important change with respect to Exchange Server 2007 is the new Database Availability Group. This will allow you to create multiple copies of an Exchange Server database within your organization, and you are no longer bound to a specific site (like in Exchange Server 2007), but can now stretch across multiple sites. Microsoft has also successfully transformed Cluster Continuous Replication and Stand-by Continuous Replication into a new Continuous Availability technology.

- While on the topic of simplifying, a lot of SysAdmins were having difficulties with the Windows Server fail-over clustering, so Microsoft has simply "removed" this from the product. The components are still there, but they are now managed using the Exchange Management Console or Exchange Management Shell.

- With the new Personal Archive ability, a user can now have a secondary mailbox, acting as a personal archive – this really is a .PST killer! You now have the ability to import all the users' .PST files and store them in the Personal Archive, and using retention policies you can move data from the primary mailbox to the archive automatically, to keep the primary mailbox at an acceptable size, *without any hassle*.

- To deal with ever-growing storage requirements, Microsoft also made considerable changes to the underlying database system. All you will need to store your database and log files with Exchange Server 2010 is a 2 TB SATA (or other Direct Attached Storage) disk. As long as you have multiple copies of the database, *you're safe*! And the maximum supported database size? That has improved from 200 GB (in an Exchange Server 2007 CCR environment) to 2 TB (in a multiple database copy Exchange Server 2010 environment). If you haven't yet considered what your business case will look like when upgrading to Exchange Server 2010, bear in mind that this will truly save a *tremendous* amount of storage cost – and that's not marketing talk!

- Installing Exchange 2010 is not at all difficult, and configuring a Database Availability Group with multiple copies of the Mailbox Databases is just a click of the mouse (you only have to be a little careful when creating multi-site DAGs). Even installing Exchange Server 2010 into an existing Exchange Server 2003 or Exchange Server 2007 environment is not that hard! The only thing you have to be aware of is the additional namespace that shows up. Besides the standard namespace like *webmail.contose.com* and *Autodiscover.contoso.com*, a third namespace shows up in a coexistence environment: *legacy.contoso.com*. This is used when you have mailboxes still on the old (i.e. Exchange Server 2003 or Exchange Server 2007) platform in a mixed environment.

- Lastly, for a die-hard GUI administrator, it might be painful to start managing an Exchange environment with the Exchange Management Shell. Basic management *can* be done with the graphical Exchange Management Console, but you really do have to use the Shell for the nitty-gritty configuration. The Shell is remarkably powerful, and it takes quite some getting used to, but with it you can do fine-grained management, and even create reports using features like output-to-HTML or save-to-.CSV file. Very neat!

I hope this book will guide you through the basic installation and configuration of Exchange Server 2010, and that the examples will give you some solid understanding of the processes involved, as well. I've certainly not provided everything; the Unified Messaging role and integration with Office Communication Server (OCS) 2007, for example, would make for some interesting additional reading. By integrating OCS 2007 R2 and Exchange Server 2010 you will not only get an interesting messaging environment, but also presence information, instant messaging (IM) functionality and integration with your voice system. All kinds of interesting topics that can be added in a second edition of this book.

If you have any comments or questions after reading this, don't hesitate to send me an email on MYBOOK@JAAPWESSELIUS.NL.

Chapter 1: Introduction to Exchange Server 2010

First things first – let's cover some basic background: Exchange Server 2010 is an email and calendaring application that runs on Windows Server 2008 and, like its predecessor Exchange Server 2007, can also integrate with your phone system. It is the seventh major version of the product and, while not revolutionary, it does include some important changes and lots of small improvements over Exchange Server 2007.

The scalability of Exchange Server 2010 has improved, especially when compared to the complex storage requirements of Exchange Server 2007. The user experience has also improved in Outlook Web App, and a lot of complex issues have seen solved, or the complexity has been removed, to make the administrator's life much easier.

In this chapter I will give a brief overview of what's changed in Exchange Server 2010, what the new features are, what features have been removed, and how it makes your life as an Exchange administrator easier.

1.1 Getting started

Exchange Server 2010 will be available in two versions:

- **Standard Edition**, which is limited to hosting 5 databases.

- **Enterprise Edition**, which can host up to 100 databases.

However, the available binaries are identical for both versions; it's the license key that establishes the difference in functionality. Exchange Server 2010 is also only available in a 64-bit version; there is absolutely no 32-bit version available, not even for testing purposes. Bear in mind that, as 64-bit-only software, there's no Itanium version of Exchange Server 2010.

Exchange Server 2010 also comes with two Client Access License (CAL) versions:

- **Standard CAL** – This license provides access to email, calendaring, Outlook Web App and ActiveSync for Mobile Devices.

- **Enterprise CAL** – This is an additive license, and provides Unified Messaging and compliance functionality, as well as Forefront Security for Exchange Server and Exchange Hosted Filtering for anti-spam and anti-virus functionality.

This is not a complete list, and for more information about licensing you can check the Microsoft website at HTTP://WWW.MICROSOFT.COM/EXCHANGE.

1.2 What's been removed from Exchange Server 2010?

As always, as new features come, old features go. There are inevitably a few that have found themselves on the "deprecated list" this time around, and so will not be continued in Exchange Server 2010 and beyond. Since this is a much shorter list than the "new features", we'll start here:

- There are some major changes in Exchange Server clustering: in Exchange Server 2007 you had **LCR** (Local Continuous Replication), **CCR** (Cluster Continuous Replication) and **SCR** (Standby Continuous Replication) – three different versions of replication, all with their own management interfaces. All three are *no longer available* in Exchange Server 2010.

- Windows **Server Fail-over Clustering** has been removed in Exchange Server 2010. Although seriously improved in Windows Server 2008, a lot of Exchange Administrators still found the fail-over clustering complex and difficult to manage. As a result, it was still prone to error and a potential source of all kinds of problems.

- **Storage Groups** are no longer available in Exchange Server 2010. The concepts of a database, log files and a checkpoint file are still there, but now it is just called a database. It's like CCR in Exchange Server 2007, where you could only have one database per Storage Group.

- Owing to major re-engineering in the Exchange Server 2010 databases, the **Single Instance Storage** (SIS) is no longer available. This means that when you send a 1 MB message to 100 recipients, the database will potentially grow by 100 MB. This will surely have an impact on the storage requirements in terms of space, but the performance improvements on the Database are really great. I'll get back on that later in this chapter.

1.3 What's new in Exchange Server 2010?

Exchange Server 2010 contains a host of improvements and a lot of new features, as well as minor changes and improvements. Over the coming sections, I'll provide an overview of the most significant updates and additions, and point you to the relevant chapters for full coverage of individual features where necessary.

1.3.1 Outlook Web App

The most visible improvement for end-users is Outlook Web App (previously known as Outlook Web Access). One of the design goals for the Outlook Web App was a seamless cross-browser experience, so users running a browser like Safari, even on an Apple MacBook, should have exactly the same user experience as users running Internet Explorer.

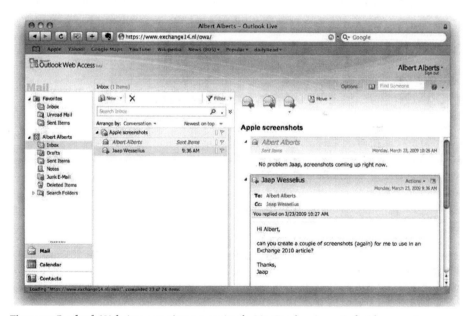

Figure 1: Outlook Web App running on an Apple MacBook using a Safari browser!

Outlook Web App offers a very rich client experience and narrows the gap between a fully-fledged Outlook client and Outlook Web Access. To reinforce that experience, a lot of new features have been introduced. To name a few: Favorites, Search Folders, attaching messages to messages, integration with Office Communicator, a new Conversation View (which works very well!), integration with SMS (text) messages and the possibility to create Outlook Web Access policies, which give the Exchange organization administrator the ability to fine-tune the user experience. The Web App is a feature which you will find mentioned throughout the book.

1.3.2 High Availability

The Exchange Server 2007 Cluster Continuous Replication (CCR) and Standby Continuous Replication (SCR) features are now combined into one new feature called **database availability**.

Database copies exist just as in an Exchange Server 2007 CCR environment and are created in a "Database Availability Group," but it is now possible to create multiple copies. The replication is not on a server level as in Exchange Server 2007 but on a database level, which gives the Exchange administrator much more fine control and granularity when it comes to creating a high available Exchange organization. The servers in such a Database Availability Group can be at the same location, or other locations to create an offsite solution. There's also no longer any need to install the Microsoft Cluster Service (MSCS) before setting up the Database Availability Group, as all cluster operations are now managed by Exchange. Chapter 5 of this book deals exclusively with all the new High Availability features of Exchange Server 2010.

1.3.3 Exchange core store functionality

Compared to Exchange Server 2003, Exchange Server 2007 dramatically decreased the I/O on the disk subsystem (sometimes by 70%). This was achieved by increasing the Exchange database page size from 4KB to 8KB and by using the 64-bit operating system. The memory scalability of the 64-bit platform makes it possible to use servers with huge amounts of memory, giving them the opportunity to cache information in memory instead of reading and writing everything to the disk.

One of the design goals of Exchange Server 2010 was to use a single 1TB SATA disk for the mailbox database *and* its log files. Another goal was to allow multi-GB mailboxes without any negative performance impact on the server. To make this possible, the database schema in Exchange Server 2010 has now been flattened, making the database structure used by the Exchange Server *much* less complex than it was in Exchange Server 2007 and earlier. As a result, the I/O requirements of an Exchange Server 2010 server can be up to 50% *less* than for the same configuration in Exchange Server 2007.

As a result of the flattened database schema, Microsoft has removed Single Instance Storage (SIS) from Exchange Server 2010, but the improvements in performance are much more significant, and more-than-adequate compensation for the (comparatively minor) loss of SIS. I'll touch upon some of these points in Chapters 2 and 3.

1.3.4 Microsoft Online Services

Microsoft is gradually moving "into the cloud." Besides an Exchange Server 2010 implementation on premise, it is now also possible to host mailboxes in a datacenter; you can host your mailboxes with your own ISP, or with Microsoft Online Services.

Exchange Server 2010 can be 100% on premise, 100% hosted, or it can be a mixed environment, with some percentage of your mailboxes hosted and the rest on premise. This is, of course, fully transparent to end-users, but it has its effects on the administration. Instead of managing just one, on-site environment, you'll have to manage the hosted organization as well. This is can all be handled through Exchange Server 2010's Exchange Management Console, where you can connect to multiple forests containing an Exchange organization.

1.3.5 New administration functionality

As a consequence of the major changes made to the High Availability features of Exchange Server 2010, the Exchange Management Console has also changed rather significantly.

Owing to the new replication functionality, the Mailbox object is no longer tied to the Exchange Server object, but is now part of the Exchange Server 2010 organization. Also, since the concept of Storage Groups is no longer relevant, their administration has been removed from both the Exchange Management Console and the Exchange Management Shell. PowerShell cmdlets like **New-StorageGroup**, **Get-StorageGroup**, and so on, have also all been removed, although the options of these cmdlets have been moved into other cmdlets, like database-related cmdlets.

Speaking of which, Exchange Server 2010 also runs on top of **PowerShell Version 2**. This version not only has a command line interface (CLI), but also an Interactive Development Environment (IDE). This enables you to easily create scripts and use variables, and you now have an output window where you can quickly view the results of your PowerShell command or script.

In addition to PowerShell V2, Exchange Server 2010 also uses **Windows Remote Management** (WinRM) Version 2. This gives you the option to remotely manage an Exchange Server 2010 server without the need to install the Exchange Management Tools on your workstation, and even via the Internet!

One last small but interesting new feature is "**Send Mail,**" allowing you to send mail directly from the Exchange Management Console – ideal for testing purposes. Chapter 4 is all about managing Exchange Server 2010, so that's where you'll find more information in this vein.

1.3.6 Exchange Control Panel

It is now possible to perform some basic Exchange management tasks using the options page in Outlook Web Access; not only on the user's own properties, but also at an organizational level. With this method, it is possible to create users, mailboxes, distribution groups, mail-enabled contact, management email addresses etc. The ECP is a big topic in Chapter 4.

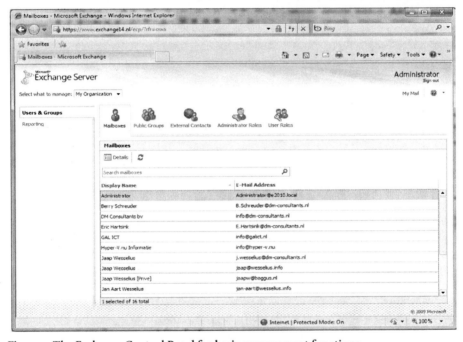

Figure 2: The Exchange Control Panel for basic management functions.

1.3.7 Active Directory Rights Management

Active Directory Rights Management Service lets you control what users can do with email and other documents that are sent to them. It is possible, for example, for classified messages to disable the "Forward" option to prevent messages being leaked outside the organization.

With Exchange Server 2010, new features have been added to the Rights Management Services, such as:

- **Integration with Transport Rules** – a template for using RMS to protect messages over the Internet.

- **RMS protection for voice mail messages** coming from the Unified Messaging Server Role.

Active Directory is discussed throughout this book, as the Exchange Server 2010 has a much closer relationship with AD than previous versions of Exchange Server.

1.3.8 Transport and routing

With Exchange Server 2010 it is possible to implement **cross premises message routing**. When using a mixed hosting environment, Exchange Server 2010 can route messages from the datacenter to the on-premise environment with full transparency.

Exchange Server 2010 also offers (at last) **enhanced disclaimers**, making it possible to add HTML content to disclaimers to add images, hyperlinks, etc. It is even possible to use Active Directory attributes (from the user's private property set) to create a personal disclaimer.

To create a highly available and reliable routing model, the Hub Transport Servers in Exchange Server 2010 now contain **Shadow Redundancy**. A message is normally stored in a database on the Hub Transport Server and, in Exchange Server 2007, the message is deleted as soon as it is sent to the next hop. In Exchange Server 2010, the message is *only* deleted after the next hop reports a successful delivery of the message. If this is not reported, the Hub Transport Server will try to resend the message.

For more High Availability messaging support, the messages stay in the transport dumpster on a Hub Transport Server, and are only deleted if they are successfully replicated to all database copies. The database on the Hub Transport Server has also been improved on an ESE level, resulting in a higher message throughput on the transport level.

1.3.9 Permissions

Previous versions of Exchange Servers relied on delegation of control via multiple Administrative Groups (specifically, Exchange Server 2000 and Exchange Server 2003) or via Group Membership. Exchange Server 2010 now contains a **Role Based Access Control** model **(RBAC)** to implement a powerful and flexible management model. I'll cover this in much more detail in Chapter 4.

1.3.10 Messaging policy and compliance

As part of a general compliance regulation, Microsoft introduced the concept of Managed Folders in Exchange Server 2007, offering the possibility to create some sort of compliancy feature. This has been enhanced with new interfaces in Exchange Server 2010, such as the option of tagging messages, cross-mailbox searches, new transport rules and actions and the new retention policies.

1.3.11 Mailbox Archive

Exchange Server 2010 now contains a personal archive; this is a secondary mailbox connected to a user's primary mailbox, and located in the same Mailbox Database as the user's primary mailbox. Since Exchange Server 2010 now supports a JBOD (Just a Bunch of Disks) configuration this isn't too big a deal, and the Mailbox Archive really is a great replacement of (locally stored) .PST files. Chapters 4 and 5 will discuss the new Mailbox Archive in more detail.

1.3.12 Unified Messaging

The Exchange Server 2010 Unified Messaging Server Role integrates a telephone system, like a PABX, with the Exchange Server messaging environment. This makes it possible to offer Outlook Voice Access, enabling you to interact with the system using your voice, listen to voice mail messages, or have messages read to you. Exchange Server 2010 offers some new functionality like **Voicemail preview**, **Messaging Waiting Indicator**, **integration with text (SMS) messages**, additional **language support**, etc. Unified Messaging is, unfortunately, a little outside the scope of this book, so you won't find me going into too much detail later on.

1.4 Exchange Server 2010 and Active Directory

As far as Active Directory is concerned, its minimum level needs to be on a Windows Server 2003 level, both for the domain functional level as well as the forest functional level. This might be confusing, since Exchange Server 2010 only runs on Windows Server 2008 or Windows Server 2008 R2, but that's just the actual server which Exchange Server 2010 is running on!

The Schema Master in the forest needs to be Windows Server 2003 SP2 server (Standard or Enterprise Edition) or higher. Likewise, in each Active Directory Site where Exchange Server 2010 will be installed, there must be *at least* one Standard or Enterprise Windows Server 2003 SP2 (or higher) server configured as a Global Catalog server.

From a performance standpoint, as with Exchange Server 2007, the ratio of 4:1 for Exchange Server processors to Global Catalog server processors still applies to Exchange Server 2010. Using a 64-bit version of Windows Server for Active Directory will naturally also increase the system performance.

Note

It is possible to install Exchange Server 2010 on an Active Directory Domain Controller. However, for performance and security reasons it is recommended not to do this, and instead to install Exchange Server 2010 on a member server in a domain.

1.4.1 Active Directory partitions

A Windows Server Active Directory consists of one forest, one or more domains and one or more sites. Exchange Server 2010 is bound to a forest, and therefore one Exchange Server 2010 Organization is connected to one Active Directory forest. The actual information in an Active Directory forest is stored in three locations, also called partitions:

- **Schema partition** – this contains a "blue print" of all objects and properties in Active Directory. In a programming scenario this would be called a class. When an object, like a user, is created, it is instantiated from the user blueprint in Active Directory.

- **Configuration partition** – this contains information that's used throughout the forest. Regardless of the number of domains that are configured in Active Directory, all domain controllers use the same Configuration Partition in that particular Active Directory forest. As such, it is replicated throughout the Active Directory forest, and all changes to the Configuration Partition have to be replicated to all Domain Controllers. All Exchange Server 2010 information is stored in the Configuration Partition.

- **Domain partition** – this contains information regarding the domains installed in Active Directory. Every domain has its own Domain Partition, so if there are 60 domains installed there will be 60 different Domain Partitions. User information, including Mailbox information, is stored in the Domain Partition.

1.4.2 Delegation of control

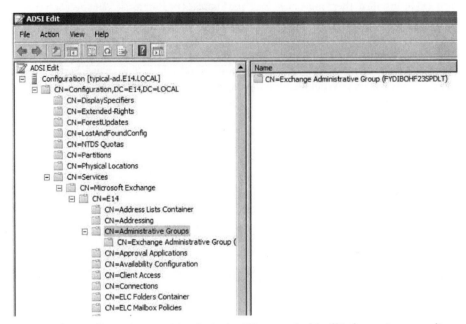

Figure 3: The Configuration partition in Active Directory holds all information regarding Exchange Server 2010 in an Administrative Group.

In Exchange Server 2003 the concept of "Administrative Groups" was used to delegate control between different groups of administrators. A default "First Administrative Group" was created during installation, and subsequent Administrative Groups could be created to install more Exchange 2003 servers and delegate control of these servers to other groups. The Administrative Groups were stored in the Configuration Partition so all domains and thus all domain controllers and Exchange servers could see them.

Exchange Server 2007 used Active Directory Security Groups for delegation of control, and only one Administrative Group is created during installation of Exchange Server 2007, called "Exchange Administrative Group – FYDIBOHF23SPDLT."[1] All servers in the organization are installed in this Administrative Group. Permissions are assigned to Security Groups and Exchange administrators are member of these Security Groups.

Exchange Server 2010 uses the same Administrative Group, but delegation of control is not done using Active Directory Security Groups, as Microsoft has introduced the concept of "Role Based Access Control" or RBAC. RBAC is covered in more detail in Chapter 4, "Managing Exchange Server 2010".

---

1   Just shift all letters in the word FYDIBOHF23SPDLT to the left and you get EXCHANGE12ROCKS.

1.4.3 Active Directory Sites

Exchange Server 2010 uses Active Directory Sites for routing messages. But what is an Active Directory site?

When a network is separated into multiple physical locations, connected with "slow" links and separated into multiple IP subnets then, in terms of Active Directory, we're talking about sites. Say, for example, there's a main office located in Amsterdam with an IP subnet of 10.10.0.0/16. There's a branch office located in London, and this location has an IP subnet of 10.11.0.0/16. Both locations have their own Active Directory Domain Controller, handling authentication for clients in their own subnet. Active Directory site links are created to control replication traffic between sites. Clients in each site use DNS to find services like Domain Controllers in their own site, thus preventing using services over the WAN link.

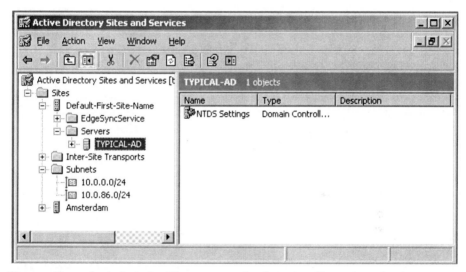

Figure 4: Two subnets in Active Directory, one for the main office and one for the Amsterdam Datacenter.

Exchange Server 2010 uses Active Directory sites for routing messages between sites. Using our current example, if there is an Exchange Server 2010 Hub Transport Server in Amsterdam and an Exchange Server 2010 Hub Transport Server in London, then the IP Site Links in Active Directory are used to route messages from Amsterdam to London. This concept was first introduced in Exchange Server 2007, and nothing has changed in Exchange Server 2010.

Exchange Server 2003 used the concept of Routing Groups, where Active Directory already used Active Directory Sites; Active Directory Sites and Exchange Server Routing Groups are not compatible with each other. To have Exchange Server 2003 and Exchange Server 2010 work together in one Exchange organization, some special connectors have to be created – the so-called Interop Routing Group Connector.

1.5 Exchange Server coexistence

It is very likely that large organizations will gradually move from an earlier version of Exchange Server to Exchange Server 2010, and Exchange Server 2010 can coexist, in the same forest, with (both) Exchange Server 2007 and Exchange Server 2003. It is also possible to move from a mixed Exchange Server 2003 and Exchange Server 2007 environment to Exchange Server 2010, as I'll discuss in Chapter 3.

Please note that it is not possible to have a coexistence scenario where Exchange Server 2000 and Exchange Server 2010 are installed in the same Exchange Organization. This is enforced in the setup of Exchange Server 2010. If the setup detects an Exchange Server 2000 installation the setup application is halted and an error is raised.

Integrating Exchange Server 2010 into an existing Exchange Server 2003 or Exchange Server 2007 environment is called a "transition" scenario. A "migration" scenario is where a new Active Directory forest is created where Exchange Server 2010 is installed. This new Active Directory forest is running in parallel with the "old" Active Directory with a previous version of Exchange Server. Special care has to be taken in this scenario, especially when both organizations coexist for any significant amount of time. Directories have to be synchronized during the coexistence phase, and the free/busy information will need to be constantly synchronized as well, since you'll still want to offer this service to users during the coexistence period.

This is a typical scenario when third-party tools like Quest are involved, although it is not clear at the time of writing this book how Quest is going to deal with Exchange Server 2010 migration scenarios.

1.6 Exchange Server 2010 server roles

Up until Exchange Server 2003, all roles were installed on one server and administrators were unable to select which features were available. It was possible to designate an Exchange 2000 or Exchange 2003 server as a so called "front-end server", but this server was just like an ordinary Exchange server acting as a protocol proxy. It still had a Mailbox Database and a Public Folder database installed by default.

Exchange Server 2007 introduced the concept of "server roles" and this concept is maintained in Exchange Server 2010. The following server roles, each with a specific function, are available in Exchange Server 2010:

- Mailbox Server (MB) role

- Client Access Server (CAS) role

- Hub Transport Server (HT) role

- Edge Transport Server (Edge) role

- Unified Messaging Server (UM) role.

These server roles can be installed on dedicated hardware, where each machine has its own role, but they can also be combined. A typical server installation, for example in the setup program, combines the Mailbox, Client Access and Hub Transport Server role. The Management Tools are always installed during installation, irrespective of which server role is installed.

By contrast, the Edge Transport Server role cannot be combined with *any* other role. In fact, the Edge Transport Server role cannot even be part of the (internal) domain, since it is designed to be installed in the network's Demilitarized Zone (DMZ).

There are multiple reasons for separating Exchange Server into multiple server roles:

- **Enhanced scalability** – since one server can be dedicated for one server role, the scalability profits are huge. This specific server can be configured and optimized for one particular Role, resulting in a high performance server.

- **Improved security** – one dedicated server can be hardened for security using the Security Configuration Wizard (SCW). Since only one Server Role is used on a particular server, all other functions and ports are disabled, resulting in a more secure system.

- **Simplified deployment and administration** – a dedicated server is easier to configure, easier to secure and easier to administer.

I will explain each server role in detail, in the following sections.

1.6.1 Mailbox Server role

The Mailbox Server role is the heart of your Exchange Server 2010 environment. This is where the Mailbox Database and Public Folder Database are installed. The sole purpose of the Mailbox Server role is to host Mailboxes and Public Folders; nothing more. In previous versions of Exchange Server, including Exchange Server 2007, Outlook clients using MAPI still connected directly to the Mailbox Server Role, but with Exchange Server 2010 this is no longer the case. MAPI clients now connect to a service called "RPC Client Access," running on the Client Access Server. (The original code name of RPC Client Access was "MAPI on the Middle Tier" or MoMT.)

The Mailbox Server Role does not route any messages, it only stores messages in mailboxes. For routing messages, the Hub Transport Server role is needed. This latter role is responsible for routing all messages, even between mailboxes that are on the same server, and even between mailboxes that are in the same mailbox database.

For accessing mailboxes, a Client Access Server is also always needed; it is just not possible to access any mailbox without a Client Access Server.

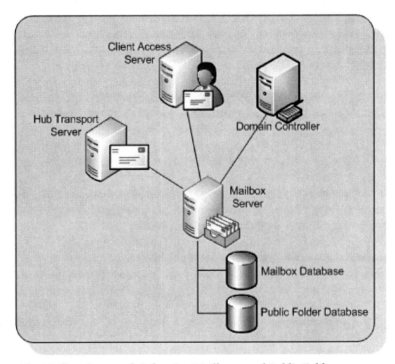

Figure 5: The Mailbox Server role is hosting Mailboxes and Public Folders.

Note that Internet Information Server is needed on a Mailbox Server role in order to implement the Role Based Access Control model (RBAC) covered in Chapter 4, even if no client is accessing the Mailbox Server directly.

As I mentioned, Storage Groups no longer exist in Exchange Server 2010, but mailboxes are still stored in databases, just like in Exchange Server 2007. Although rumors have been circulating for more than ten years that the database engine used in Exchange Server will be replaced by a SQL Server engine, it has not happened yet. Just as in earlier versions of Exchange Server, the Extensible Storage Engine (ESE) is still being used, although major changes have been made to the database and the database schema.

By default, the first database on a server will be installed in the directory:

```
C:\Program Files\ Microsoft\Exchange Server\V14\Mailbox\Mailbox
Database <<identifier>>
```

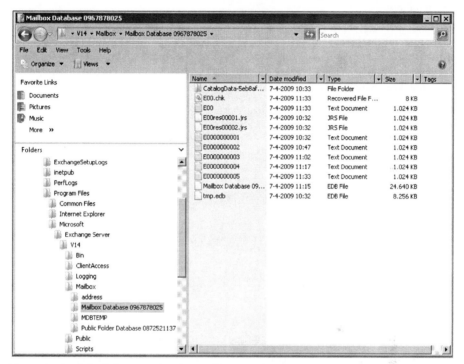

Figure 6: The default location for the Mailbox Databases and the log files.

The <<identifier>> is a unique number to make sure that the Mailbox Database name is unique within the Exchange organization.

It is best practice, from both a performance and a recovery perspective, to place the database and the accompanying log files on a dedicated disk. This disk can be on a Fiber Channel SAN, on an iSCSI SAN, or on a Direct Attached Storage (DAS) solution. Whilst it was a design goal to limit the amount of disk I/O to a level where both the database and the log files could be installed on a 1TB SATA disk, this is only an option if Database Copies are configured and you have at least two copies of the Mailbox Database, in order to avoid a single point of failure.

1.6.2 Client Access Server role

The Client Access Server role offers access to the mailboxes for all available protocols. In Exchange Server 2003, Microsoft introduced the concept of "front-end" and "back-end" servers, and the Client Access Server role is comparable to an Exchange Server 2003 front-end server.

All clients connect to the Client Access Server and, after authentication, the requests are proxied to the appropriate Mailbox Server. Communication between the client and the Client Access Server is via the normal protocols (HTTP, IMAP4, POP3 and MAPI), and communication between the Client Access Server and the Mailbox Server is via Remote Procedure Calls (RPC).

The following functionality is provided by the Exchange Server 2010 Client Access Server:

*   HTTP for Outlook Web App

*   Outlook Anywhere (formerly known as RPC/HTTP) for Outlook 2003, Outlook 2007 and Outlook 2010

*   ActiveSync for (Windows Mobile) PDAs

*   Internet protocols POP3 and IMAP4

*   RPC Client Access (formerly MoMT)

*   Availability Service, Autodiscover and Exchange Web Services – these services are offered to Outlook 2007 clients and provide free/busy information, automatic configuration of the Outlook 2007 and Outlook 2010 client, the Offline Address Book downloads and Out-of-Office functionality.

....

Note

SMTP Services are not offered by the Client Access Server. All SMTP Services are handled by the Hub Transport Server.

....

At least one Client Access Server is needed for each Mailbox Server in an Active Directory site, as well as a fast connection between the Client Access Server and the Mailbox Server. The Client Access Server also needs a fast connection to a Global Catalog Server.

The Client Access Server should be deployed on the internal network and NOT in the network's Demilitarized Zone (DMZ). In order to access a Client Access Server from the

Internet, a Microsoft Internet Security and Acceleration (ISA) Server should be installed in the DMZ. All necessary Exchange services should be "published" to the Internet, on this ISA Server.

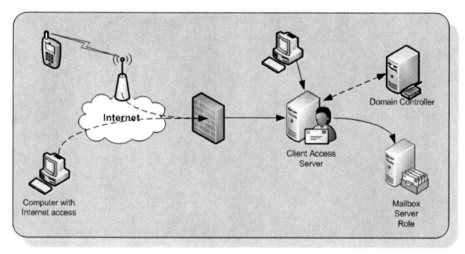

Figure 7: The Client Access Server is responsible for providing access to (Internet) clients. The ISA Server is not in this picture.

1.6.3 Hub Transport Server role

The Hub Transport Server role is responsible for routing messaging, not only between the Internet and the Exchange organization, but also between Exchange servers within your organization.

All messages are always routed via the Hub Transport Server role, even if the source and the destination mailbox are on the same server, and even if the source and the destination mailbox are in the same Mailbox Database. For example, in Figure 8, the Hub Transport Server is responsible for routing all messages:

Step 1: A message is sent to the Hub Transport Server.

Step 2: A recipient on the same server as the sender means the message is sent back.

Step 3: When the recipient is on another mailbox server, the message is routed to the appropriate Hub Transport Server. This is then followed by...

...Step 4: The second Hub Transport Server delivers the message to the Mailbox Server of the recipient.

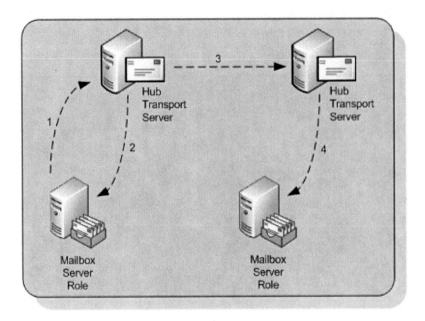

Figure 8: The Hub Transport Server is responsible for routing all messages.

The reason for routing all messages through the Hub Transport Server is simply compliancy. Using the Hub Transport Server, it is possible to track all messaging flowing through the Exchange organization and to take appropriate action if needed (legal requirements, HIPAA, Sarbanes-Oxley, and so on). On the Hub Transport Server the following agents can be configured for compliancy purposes:

- **Transport Rule agents** – using Transport Rules, all kinds of actions can be applied to messages according to the Rule's filter or conditions. Rules can be applied to internal messages, external messages or both.

- **Journaling agents** – using the journaling agent, it is possible to save a copy of every message sent or received by a particular recipient.

Since a Mailbox Server does not deliver any messages, every Mailbox Server in an Active Directory site requires a Hub Transport Server in that site. The Hub Transport Server also needs a fast connection to a Global Catalog server for querying Active Directory. This Global Catalog server should be in the same Active Directory site as the Hub Transport Server.

When a message has an external destination, i.e. a recipient on the Internet, the message is sent from the Hub Transport Server to the "outside world." This may be via an Exchange Server 2010 Edge Transport Server in the DMZ, but the Hub Transport Server can also deliver messages directly to the Internet.

Optionally, the Hub Transport Server can be configured to deal with anti-spam and anti-virus functions. The anti-spam services are not enabled on a Hub Transport Server by default, since this service is intended to be run on an Edge Transport Service in the DMZ. Microsoft has supplied a script on every Hub Transport Server that can be used to enable their anti-spam services if necessary.

Anti-virus services can be achieved by installing the Microsoft Forefront for Exchange software. The anti-virus software on the Hub Transport Server will scan inbound and outbound SMTP traffic, whereas anti-virus software on the Mailbox Server will scan the contents of a Mailbox Database, providing a double layer of security.

1.6.4 Edge Transport Server (Edge) role

The Edge Server role was introduced with Exchange Server 2007, and provides an extra layer of message hygiene. The Edge Transport Server role is typically installed as an SMTP gateway in the network's "Demilitarized Zone" or DMZ. Messages from the Internet are delivered to the Edge Transport Server role and, after anti-spam and anti-virus services, the messages are forwarded to a Hub Transport Server on the internal network.

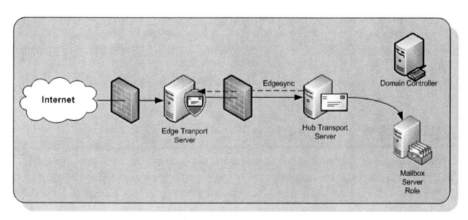

Figure 9: The Edge Transport Server is installed between the Internet and the Hub Transport Server.

The Edge Transport Server can also provide the following services:

- **Edge Transport Rules** – like the Transport Rules on the Hub Transport Server, these rules can also control the flow of messages that are sent to, or received from, the Internet when they meet a certain condition.

- **Address rewriting** – with address rewriting, the SMTP address of messages sent to, or received from, the Internet can be changed. This can be useful for hiding internal domains, for example after a merger of two companies, but before one Active Directory and Exchange organization is created.

The Edge Transport Server is installed in the DMZ and cannot be a member of the company's internal Active Directory and Exchange Server 2010 organization. The Edge Transport Server uses the Active Directory Lightweight Directory Services (AD LDS) to store all information. In previous versions of Windows this service was called Active Directory Application Mode (ADAM). Basic information regarding the Exchange infrastructure is stored in the AD LDS, like the recipients and the Hub Transport Server to which the Edge Transport Server is sending its messages.

To keep the AD LDS database up to date, a synchronization feature called Edgesync is used, which pushes information from the Hub Transport Server to the Edge Transport Server at regular intervals.

1.6.5 Unified Messaging Server role

The Exchange Server 2010 Unified Messaging Server role combines the mailbox database and both voice messages and email messages into one store. Using the Unified Messaging Server role it is possible to access all messages in the mailbox using either a telephone or a computer.

The phone system can be an IP-based system or a "classical" analog PBX system although, in the latter case, a special Unified Messaging IP Gateway is needed to connect the two.

The Unified Messaging Server role provides users with the following features:

- **Call Answering** – this feature acts as an answering machine. When somebody cannot answer the phone, a personal message can be played after which a caller can leave a message. The message will be recorded and sent to the recipient's mailbox as an .mp3 file.

- **Subscriber Access** – sometimes referred to as "Outlook Voice Access." Using Subscriber Access, users can access their mailbox using a normal phone line and listen to their voicemail messages. It is also possible to access regular mailbox items like messages and calendar items, and even reschedule appointments in the calendar.

- **Auto Attendant** – using the Auto Attendant, it is possible to create a custom menu in the Unified Messaging system using voice prompts. A caller can use either the telephone keypad or his or her voice to navigate through the menu.

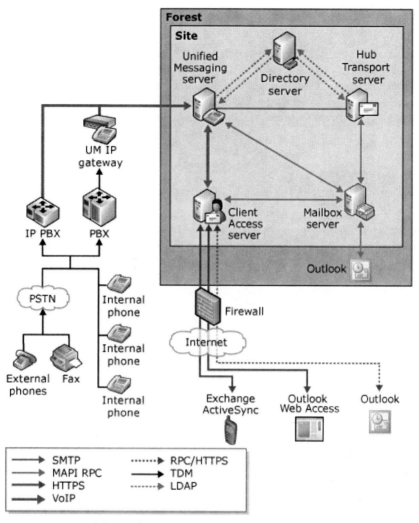

Figure 10: Overview of the Unified Messaging Infrastructure.

The Unified Messaging service installed on the Unified Messaging Server role works closely with the Microsoft Exchange Speech Engine Service. This Speech Engine Service provides the following services:

- **Dual Tone Multi Frequency (DTMF)** also referred to as the touch-tone (the beeps you hear when dialing a phone number or accessing a menu).

- Automatic Speech Recognition.

- **Text-to-Speech** service that's responsible for reading mailbox items and reading the voice menus.

The Unified Messaging Server role should be installed in an Active Directory site together with a Hub Transport Server, since this latter server is responsible for routing messaging to the Mailbox Servers. It also should have a fast connection to a Global Catalog server. If possible, the Mailbox Server role should be installed as close as possible to the Unified Messaging Server role, preferably in the same site and with a decent network connection.

1.7 Summary

Exchange Server 2010 is the new Messaging and Collaboration platform from Microsoft, and it has a lot of new, compelling features. The new High Availability, management and compliancy features make Exchange Server 2010 a very interesting product for the Exchange administrator. In fact, the new features in Exchange Server 2010 will generally result in *less* complexity, which is always a good thing!

In the next chapter, I will give you a more detailed walk-through about installing Exchange Server 2010.

Chapter 2: Installing Exchange Server 2010

In the previous chapter, I took you through a brief description of what's new in Exchange Server 2010, and what has been removed from the product. Now it's time to install Exchange Server 2010 and get a handle on the real look-and-feel. In this chapter we will Install Exchange Server 2010 in a "greenfield" scenario, meaning we'll be working with a fresh Active Directory environment, and the Exchange Server 2010 organization we'll install will be the first Exchange installation in that environment. This chapter will be a fairly straightforward, step-by-step guide to the installation process, and will cover both the prerequisites of the installation environment and the post-installation configuration of various features. In short, you should have everything you need here to get up and running, and I'll refer to aspects of this process when I take you through coexistence with Exchange Server 2003 and 2007 in the next chapter.

So, before installing Exchange Server 2010, several prerequisites have to be met.

- Exchange Server 2010 **only** runs on Windows Server 2008 and Windows Server 2008 R2. Since Windows Server 2008 also needs some additional software to be installed, and bearing in mind the improvements in Windows Server 2008 R2, the latter is the better option.

- Any Active Directory domain containing Exchange objects has to be running in (at the very least) Windows 2003 domain functional level.

- The Active Directory forest also has to be running in at least Windows 2003 forest functional level.

- The Schema Master and the Global Catalog Server(s) have to have a minimum level of Windows Server 2003 R2.

- Exchange Server 2010 **cannot** be installed in an organization where an Exchange Server 2000 exists.

2.1 Installing the Exchange Server 2010 prerequisites

When installing Exchange Server 2010 on Windows Server 2008, some additional software needs to be installed first:

- .NET Framework 3.5.

- Windows PowerShell 2.0 – An update for the MMC Snap as described in knowledge article 951725 (HTTP://TINYURL.COM/UPDATEMMC).

- The ASP .NET Ajax extensions (HTTP://TINYURL.COM/AJAXEXT).

- Internet Information Server 7.0.

- The Office 2007 Filter Pack (for the Hub Transport Server and Mailbox Server Role).

The installation program will give you the option to install .NET 3.5 and PowerShell V2 when you begin the installation, but you'll need to install the rest of the prerequisites yourself. The Internet Information Server software is now also needed on *all* the server roles of Exchange Server 2010, but there are some more fine-grained differences between the various server roles, as you can see in the following table:

Description	Mgmt Tools	Mailbox	Hub Transport	Client Access	UM	Edge
.NET Framework 3.5	Yes	Yes	Yes	Yes	Yes	Yes
PowerShell 2.0	Yes	Yes	Yes	Yes	Yes	Yes
Windows Remote Management	Yes	Yes	Yes	Yes	Yes	Yes
Hot fix kb 951725	Yes	Yes	Yes	Yes	Yes	Yes
MS Filter Pack		Yes				
ServerManagerCmd -i Web-Server		Yes	Yes	Yes	Yes	
ServerManagerCmd -i Web-Metabase	Yes	Yes	Yes	Yes	Yes	
ServerManagerCmd -i Web-Lgcy-Mgmt-Console	Yes	Yes	Yes	Yes	Yes	

Description	Mgmt Tools	Mailbox	Hub Transport	Client Access	UM	Edge
ServerManagerCmd -i Web-Basic-Auth		Yes	Yes	Yes	Yes	
ServerManagerCmd -i Web-Windows-Auth		Yes	Yes	Yes	Yes	
ServerManagerCmd -i Web-Net-Ext		Yes	Yes	Yes	Yes	
ServerManagerCmd -i Web-Digest-Auth				Yes		
ServerManagerCmd -i Web-Dyn-Compression				Yes		
ServerManagerCmd -i NET-HTTP-Activation				Yes		
ServerManagerCmd -i Web-ISAPI-Ext				Yes		
ServerManagerCmd -i RPC-over-HTTP-proxy (only needed for Outlook Anywhere)				Yes		
ServerManagerCmd -i Desktop-Experience					Yes	
ServerManagerCmd -i ADLDS						Yes
ServerManagerCmd -i Failover-Clustering (only needed for Database Availability)		Yes				
ServerManagerCmd -i RSAT-ADDS	Yes	Yes	Yes	Yes	Yes	

Table 1: Internet Information Server settings for all Exchange Server 2010 server roles.

If you want to install the Exchange Server 2010 Management Tools on a Windows Vista workstation, you'll have to install the following software:

- .NET Framework 3.5.

- Windows PowerShell 2.0.

- An update for the MMC Snap-in as described in knowledge article 951725 (HTTP://TINYURL.COM/UPDATEMMC).

- Some basic parts of the Internet Information Server: the IIS Web Metabase and the IIS Legacy Management Console.

Note

When installing Exchange Server 2010 on a Windows Server 2008 R2 server, almost all the prerequisite software is already included in the product. You only have to install Windows Server 2008 R2, install Internet Information Server (as outlined below), and you're ready to go!

The .NET Framework 3.5 can be automatically downloaded the first time you use Windows Update, but do *not* install PowerShell using the Windows Server 2008 Server Manager. This installs PowerShell Version 1, and Exchange Server 2010 needs PowerShell Version 2, which you can download from the Microsoft website.

The various configurations of Internet Information Server 7 can be easily installed using the ServerManagerCmd.exe application, which is a command-line version of the Windows Server 2008 Server Manager. To make it possible to change the Active Directory schema on a non-domain controller before this process, enter the following command on the server you want to install Exchange Server 2010 on:

```
ServerManagerCmd -i RSAT-ADDS[1]
```

Note

When the –Restart option is added to ServerManagerCmd.exe the server will automatically restart as necessary.

---

[1]   This command installs the LDIFDE program on the server, making it possible to make schema changes during setup of Exchange Server 2010.

This command will add the Active Directory Management tools on your Windows 2008 Server to make it possible to change the Active Directory Schema from this particular server.

Once that process is finished, enter these commands to install the various components of Internet Information Server 7:

```
ServerManagerCmd -i Web-Server
ServerManagerCmd -i Web-ISAPI-Ext
ServerManagerCmd -i Web-Metabase
ServerManagerCmd -i Web-Lgcy-Mgmt-Console
ServerManagerCmd -i Web-Basic-Auth
ServerManagerCmd -i Web-Digest-Auth
ServerManagerCmd -i Web-Windows-Auth
ServerManagerCmd -i Web-Dyn-Compression
ServerManagerCmd -i Web-Net-Ext
ServerManagerCmd -i RPC-over-HTTP-proxy (when Outlook
          Anywhere is used)
ServerManagerCmd -i Net-HTTP-Activation
ServerManagerCmd -i Desktop-Experience (when the UM role is
          required)
```

If you want to speed up the process, or your fingers get tired and you don't want to enter that many commands, you can enter various options in one ServerManagerCmd cmdlet, like this:

```
ServerManagerCmd -i Web-Server Web-ISAPI-Ext Web-Metabase Web-
Lgcy-Mgmt-Console Web-Basic-Auth Web-Digest-Auth Web-Windows-Auth
Web-Dyn-Compression Web-Net-Ext RPC-over-HTTP-proxy Net-HTTP-
Activation Desktop-Experience
```

Just make sure you change these commands according to the information in Table 1.

And here's some more good news: Microsoft makes an Exchange Administrator's life easier! With Exchange Server 2010, Microsoft supplies a number of XML files (one for every server role) that automate all prerequisite software installation.

Navigate to the \scripts directory on the installation media; there you'll find a number of **XML files, like Exchange-Hub.XML, Exchange-CAS.XML and Exchange-MBX.XML. These** can be used as an input file for the ServerManagerCmd.exe application.

To install the prerequisite software for a typical Exchange 2010 Server installation, just enter the following command:

```
ServerManagerCmd.exe -InputPath Exchange-Typical.XML
```

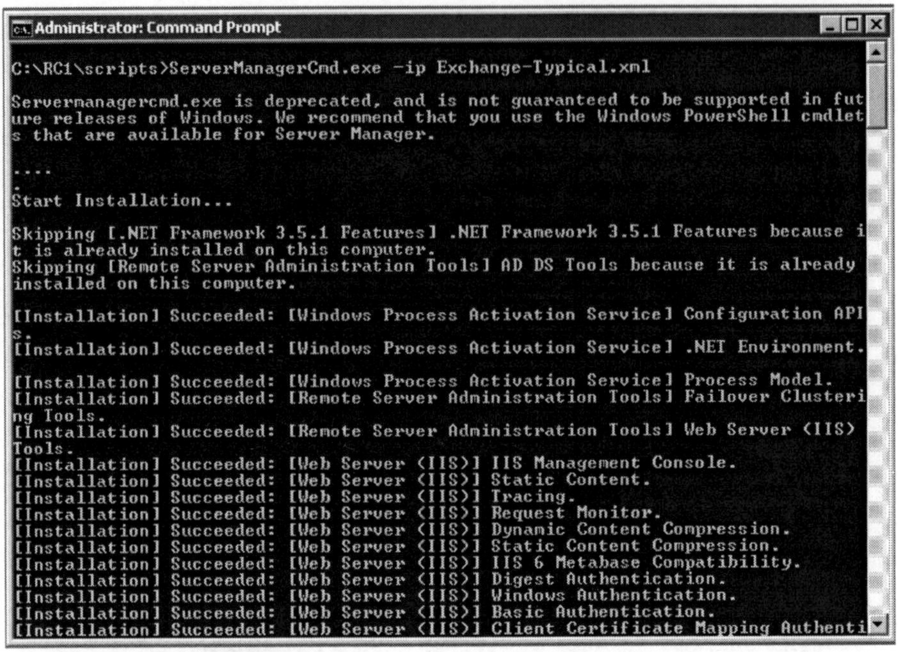

Figure 1: The installation of the prerequisite software is fully automated.

Most of the Exchange Server 2010 server roles can be combined on a single server, just as in Exchange Server 2007. Specifically, the Mailbox Server, Client Access Server, Hub Transport Server and Unified Messaging Server can be installed together on one machine. However, none of these server roles can be installed alongside the Exchange Server 2010 Edge Transport Server role, as this is a completely standalone role. I'll cover the installation of the Exchange Server 2010 Edge Transport Server role in Section 7.

2.2 Performing a typical Exchange Server 2010 install

When performing a typical server install, the account that's used for the installation process needs to be a member of the Schema Administrators group in Active Directory, as well as a member of the Enterprise Administrators. This is true for an upgrade *as well as* a completely new installation.

To install Exchange Server 2010, just follow these steps:

1. Log on to the server on which you want to install Exchange Server 2010.

2. Navigate to the installation (DVD, local directory or a network share) and double-click the setup.exe program. This will start the setup splash-screen.

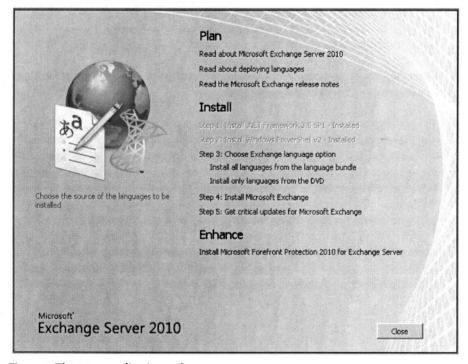

Plan

Read about Microsoft Exchange Server 2010

Read about deploying languages

Read the Microsoft Exchange release notes

Install

Step 1: Install .NET Framework 3.5 SP1 - Installed

Step 2: Install Windows PowerShell v2 - Installed

Step 3: Choose Exchange language option

    Install all languages from the language bundle

    Install only languages from the DVD

Step 4: Install Microsoft Exchange

Step 5: Get critical updates for Microsoft Exchange

Enhance

Install Microsoft Forefront Protection 2010 for Exchange Server

Choose the source of the languages to be installed

Microsoft®
Exchange Server 2010

Close

Figure 2: The setup application welcome screen.

3. If you haven't already installed the Exchange Server 2010 prerequisites, the setup program offers the possibility to install them using the menu.

    a. Install Microsoft .NET Framework 3.5

    b. Install Windows PowerShell V2 .

4. You have to select the Language Options for Exchange Server 2010. You can download all Language files from the Language Bundle (locally stored or on the Internet) or continue with the Language that's on your DVD. If you select this option, only the default language will be used. Not only for the setup application, but also, for example, for the Outlook Web App.

5. When all prerequisite software is installed you can select "*Step 4: Install Microsoft Exchange.*"

6. On the Introduction and Confirmation Pages you can just click Next after you've read the messages.

7. You'll need to "accept the terms in the license agreement" – select the appropriate radio button and click Next.

8. Depending on your company policy, select whether or not you want to enable the Error Reporting feature and click Next to continue.

9. The next page asks for the Installation Type. You can select a typical Exchange Server installation, where the Hub Transport Server role, Client Access Server role, Mailbox Server role and the Exchange Management Tools are all installed on the same server. The second option is a custom Exchange Server installation, where you can select which individual roles to install.

10. Select the Typical Exchange Server Installation and click Next to continue.

11. Since this is a fresh installation, an Exchange organization doesn't exist yet, so you'll need to enter a name for the Exchange Server organization. The default name is "First Organization," but any name can be used as long as these are the only characters used:

    • A through Z

    • a through z

    • 0 through 9

    • Space (not leading or trailing)

    • Hyphen or dash.

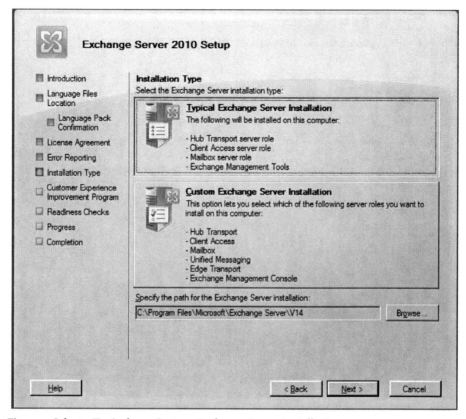

Figure 3: Select a Typical or a Custom Exchange Server installation.

Throughout this book I'll use the organization name "E14." Click Next once you've entered a valid organization name.

12. The next window is the Client Settings window, and this is very important. Your selection needs to be based on the email clients used in your organization. Outlook 2003 or earlier and Entourage clients depend on Public Folders for Free/Busy information (i.e. calendaring) and Offline Address Book downloads. On the other hand, Outlook 2007 and Outlook 2010 can both use the Availability Services and Web-based Offline Address Book Download features in Exchange Server 2007 and later. If you do not install Public Folders at this time, it's always possible to install Public Folders later to support Outlook 2003 or Entourage clients in your Exchange environment. Click Next to continue.

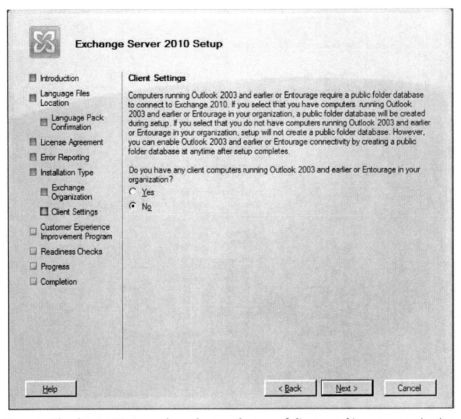

Figure 4: The client settings are dependent on the type of clients used in your organization.

13. A new aspect of the Exchange Server 2010 setup process is the option to enter the external domain name. If you *do* enter an external domain name, the Exchange Server 2010 Client Access Server role will be configured smoothly and automatically with the appropriate settings. If you do not enter an external domain name during the setup, you'll have to configure the settings manually after the setup has finished.

14. Depending on your company policy, you can choose whether or not to join the Exchange Customer Experience Improvement Program, and then click Next.

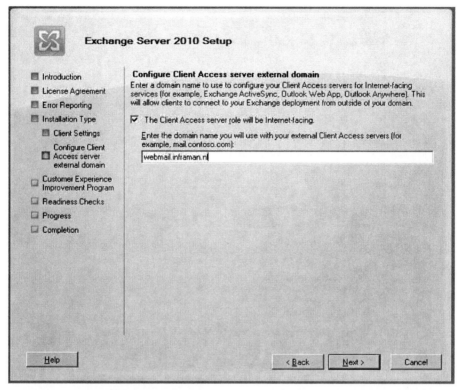

Figure 5: Enter the External Domain Name for automatically configuring the Client Access Server.

15. The next step is the Readiness Check. The setup program will run a final check on the server's readiness for the Exchange organization, the language packs and the server roles. If any prerequisite is missing, it's displayed here and you'll have the option to correct the issues. If all the checks come back OK, you can finally click that inviting "Install" button.

16. During the installation, the progress is shown for each part of the process. This whole affair can take a considerable amount of time, depending on the hardware being used for the Exchange Server, so you'll need to be patient. Once the setup program is finished you'll have the option to view the setup log, just in case of problems (which, if you've followed these steps, there shouldn't be). When you click on "Finish," the setup program is done, and the Exchange Management Console is opened to finalize the new Exchange server.

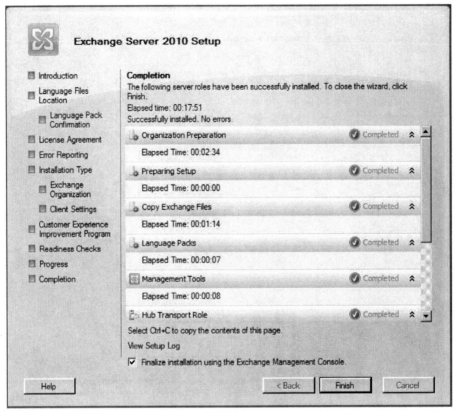

Figure 6: When the setup program is finished it can be finalized using the Exchange Management Console.

2.3 Unattended setup

It is also possible to install Exchange Server 2010 fully unattended. This may be useful when installing multiple servers, since unattended setup is actually *less* prone to errors. This process assumes that all the prerequisite software has been installed, including Internet Information Server and the LDIFDE program (HTTP://TINYURL.COM/LDIFDE) to prepare the Schema.

2.3.1 PrepareSchema

The first step in an unattended setup is to prepare the schema. This basically means upgrading the schema to an Exchange Server 2010 level. Several Exchange-related objects and attributes are added to the Active Directory schema, which can take a considerable amount of time. You'll need to be patient, again.

To prepare the schema, log on to the server as an administrator who is a member of both the Schema Admins and Enterprise Admins Security Groups. Open a command prompt, navigate to the Exchange Server 2010 installation media and type the following command:

```
Setup.com /PrepareSchema
```

The command line setup program will start and upgrade the Active Directory schema to an Exchange Server 2010 level. If you have multiple Domain Controllers, wait until the schema changes have been replicated to all Domain Controllers in the forest *before* continuing with the next step.

2.3.2 PrepareAD

After preparing the Schema, **Active Directory** now has to be prepared for Exchange Server 2010 because, as I explained in Chapter 1, the Exchange Server 2010 organization is installed in the Configuration Partition of Active Directory. This is why the account used for the installation needs to be a member of the Enterprise Admins Security Group (Domain Administrators cannot write in the Configuration Partition).

Log on to the server, open a command prompt and navigate to the Exchange Server 2010 installation media, and type this command:

```
Setup.com /PrepareAD /OrganizationName:E14
```

The Active Directory Configuration Partition will now be prepared for Exchange Server 2010 using the previously-mentioned "E14" Organization name.

Figure 7: Preparing the Active Directory Configuration Partition for Exchange Server 2010.

Please note the warning during setup; if you create an Exchange Server 2010 organization, you are not able to add any Exchange Server 2007 server roles to it!

If you want to check the creation of the Exchange Server 2010 organization you can use ADSIEdit (see Figure 8) and navigate to the Configuration container. Open CN=Configuration > CN=Services > CN=Microsoft Exchange. Right here, a new entry CN=E14 holding the Exchange Server 2010 configuration should be created.

If you have multiple Domain Controllers, wait until the Schema changes have been replicated to all Domain Controllers in the forest *before* continuing with the next step.

2.3.3 PrepareDomain

The last step in preparing the Active Directory environment is to prepare the domain that is going to host Exchange Server 2010.

Log on to the server using an administrator account, open a command prompt and navigate to the Exchange Server 2010 installation media. Type the following command:

```
Setup.com /PrepareDomain
```

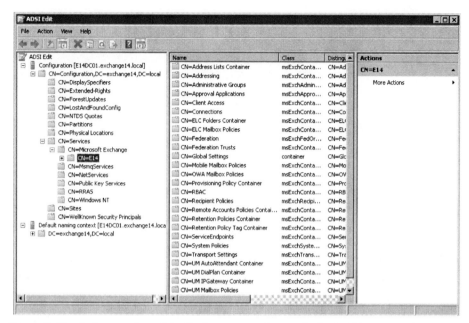

Figure 8: Check the creation of the Exchange organization in Active Directory using ADSIEdit.

The current domain will now be prepared for the introduction of Exchange Server 2010. If you want to prepare all domains in the forest for Exchange Server 2010, you can also use the /PrepareAllDomains switch.

During the preparation of the domain, a container is created in the root of the domain called "Microsoft Exchange Security Groups." This container holds the following Security Groups:

- Exchange all hosted organizations

- Exchange organization administrators

- Exchange Public Folder administrators

- Exchange Recipient Administrators

- Exchange Self-Service users

- Exchange Servers

- Exchange Trusted Subsystem

- Exchange view-only administrators.

- Exchange Windows permissions.

- ExchangeLegacyInterop.

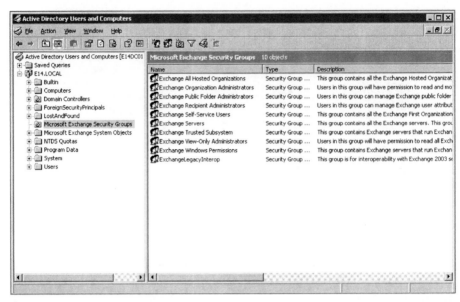

Figure 9: The Security Groups created after preparing the domain for Exchange Server 2010.

When the preparation of the domain (or indeed domains) is finished, just make sure you wait until replication to all the Domain Controllers is finished.

2.3.4 Install server roles

The very last step is to install the actual server roles. This can be done using the setup.com program with the /mode and /roles switches. The /mode switch is used to select the "install" option, the /roles switch is used to select which server roles are installed.

For an unattended typical server setup, log on to the server and open a command prompt. Navigate to the Exchange Server 2010 installation media (one last time) and enter the following command:

```
Setup.com /mode:install /roles:ht,ca,mb
```

The Exchange Server 2010 Hub Transport Server, Client Access Server and Mailbox Server roles will now be installed in the default location, which is C:\Program Files\Microsoft\Exchange\v14.

When entered, the following will be shown on the screen:

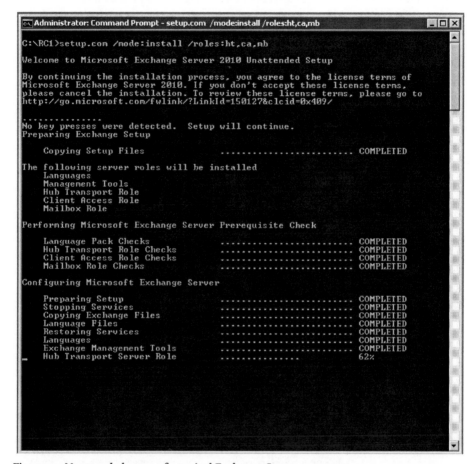

Figure 10: Unattended setup of a typical Exchange Server 2010 server.

2.4 Check the Exchange installation

After installing Exchange Server 2010, it's time to check if that installation was successful.

To start with, you should have noticed if anything went wrong during the installation because an error message would have been raised, and the setup program would probably have aborted. If not, the installation program finished successfully.

Check if you can log on using Outlook Web App by typing HTTPS://LOCALHOST/OWA into your web browser. When Exchange Server 2010 is running fine, you should first see a certificate error message. This is normal behavior the first time you log on; it's because if the Client Access Server is installed, a self-signed certificate comes along with it. This security certificate is not issued by a trusted certificate authority, hence the error, but in this case it is safe to continue. A logon page should be presented and, after entering the Administrator's credentials, you should have access to the Administrator's mailbox as shown in Figure 11.

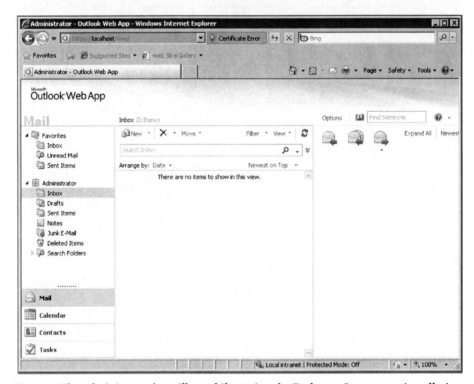

Figure 11:The Administrator's mailbox while testing the Exchange Server 2010 installation.

You can also check the Services MMC snap-in on the newly installed Exchange server. It should contain all Exchange services as shown in Figure 12.

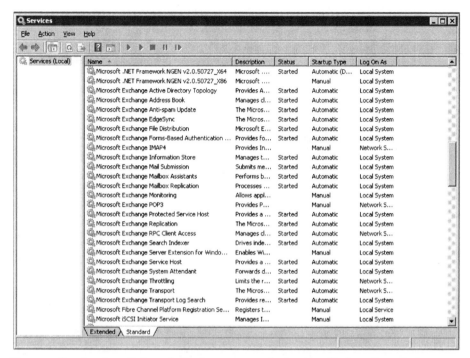

Figure 12: Services installed on the Exchange server during installation of a typical server.

The last step is to check the event log of the Exchange server, and this should not give any indications that something went wrong during the installation.

2.5 Installing dedicated server roles

For scalability and availability reasons it can be useful to separate the various Exchange Server 2010 server roles onto different machines, giving you dedicated Mailbox Servers, Hub Transport Servers, Client Access Servers and Unified Messaging Servers. I'll cover the benefits of this kind of setup later in the book.

The prerequisites for a dedicated Exchange Server 2010 installation are exactly the same as for a typical installation with multiple roles installed on one server. Just make sure you follow the guidelines from Table 1 to install the proper parts of Internet Information Server for the server role you want.

When installing a dedicated Exchange Server 2010 Mailbox Server role, start the setup.exe application from the installation media and, when reaching the "Installation Type" window, you should now select the "Custom Exchange Server installation." At this stage you'll be able to select the Server Role you want (such as, for example the "Mailbox Role" as can be seen in Figure 13).

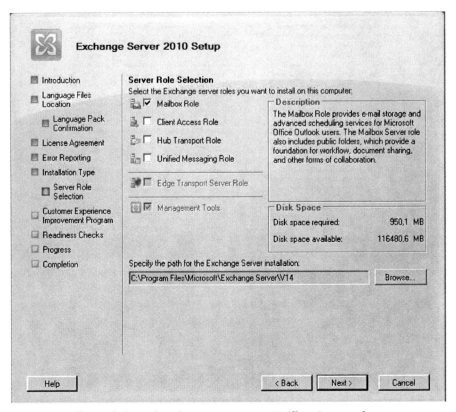

Figure 13: Installing a dedicated Exchange Server 2010 Mailbox Server role.

It is also possible to install a dedicated server role using the command line setup. When entering the setup command, just use the appropriate switch to enter the roles you want to install. For example, if you want to install the Mailbox Server role using the command line setup, enter the following command:

```
Setup.com /mode:install /roles:mb
```

2.6 Installing the Edge Transport Server

In order to offer Exchange services, the Edge Transport Server has a local copy of the most significant information of the company's Active Directory. This is stored in a Lightweight Directory Services database, which was formerly known as "Active Directory Application Mode" or ADAM. This database only stores a subset of the Active Directory information, and only informational items like recipients that exist in the internal Exchange organization. No information is stored that can compromise the company's Active Directory security.

Note

The Edge Transport Server should never be a member of the forest that holds the Exchange organization.

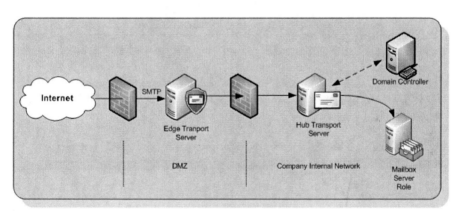

Figure 14: The Edge Transport Server located in the DMZ.

Being in the DMZ (demilitarized zone), the Exchange Server 2010 Edge Transport Server role does not have full access to the corporate network, so it does not have access to the corporate Domain Controllers, and since the Edge Transport Server is in the DMZ, it cannot use the company's internal DNS servers, and so needs to use external DNS servers instead. The Edge Transport Server must always be able to resolve external SMTP hosts for delivering messages, hence the external DNS server entries.

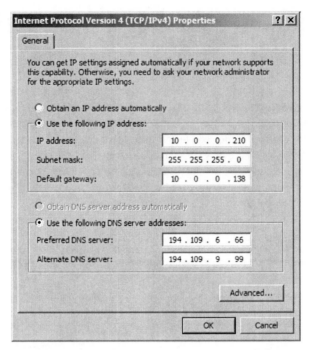

Figure 15: External DNS Settings on the network interface of the Edge Transport Server.

As part of its role, the Edge Transport Server also needs to deliver SMTP messages to the internal Hub Transport Server. To resolve these servers, they have to be added to the Edge Transport Server's HOSTS file.

Being in the DMZ (and therefore *not* a part of the internal domain) the Edge Transport Server's DNS Suffix has to be configured manually. To do this, follow the steps below.

1. Open the properties of "My Computer" on the Edge Transport Server.

2. Select Computer Name and click on the Change button.

3. On the Computer Name tab click the More button.

4. In the "Primary DNS Suffix for this computer" enter your external DNS Suffix.

5. Click OK and reboot your computer.

As can be derived from Figure 1, the Exchange Server 2010 Edge Transport Server role has the following prerequisites:

- .NET Framework 3.5

- PowerShell 2.0

- Active Directory Lightweight Directory Services.

2.6.1 Installing Active Directory Lightweight Directory Services

The Active Directory Lightweight Directory Services (AD LDS), previously known as Active Directory Application Mode or ADAM, can be installed using the Windows Server 2008 Server Manager. To install the AD LDS follow the steps below.

1. Log on to the server, click the Start button and select the Server Manager.

2. In the Server Manager, click "Roles" and in the action click "Add Roles."

3. Click Next on the "before you begin" page.

4. On the "select server role" page, select the "Active Directory Lightweight Directory Services" and click Next.

5. On the Introduction page, click Next.

6. On the Confirmation page, click Install.

7. On the Installation Results page, click Finish.

The Active Directory Lightweight Directory Services role is now installed and the server is ready for the Edge Server Role.

2.6.2 Installing the Edge Transport Server role

When all the prerequisite software for the Exchange Server 2010 Edge Transport Server role is installed, you can move on to the Exchange server itself.

1. Log on to the server with local administrator credentials, go to the installation media and start the setup.exe installation program.

2. Once all prerequisite software is installed correctly, the first two options are grayed out and you can directly select "Install Exchange Server 2010."

3. On the Introduction Page click Next.

4. Accept the License Agreement and click Next.

5. Select whether or not you want to participate in the Error Reporting Feature and click Next.

6. On the Installation Type page select "Custom Installation" and click Next. If needed, you can select another directory where the Exchange software is installed.

7. On the Server Role Selection page select the Edge Transport Server role. Notice that when you select this role the other roles (Mailbox, Client Access, etc.) are grayed out immediately. Click Next to continue.

8. The setup program will now perform a readiness to check to see if your server is capable of running the Edge Transport Server role. When successfully completed click Install to continue.

9. The Exchange binaries will now be copied to the local disk, the Management Tools will be installed and the Edge Transport Server will be installed. This can take quite some time to finish.

10. When finished you can continue configuring the Edge Transport Server using the Exchange Management Console.

The Edge Transport Server is now installed, but not yet configured. It is possible to configure everything, like the Accepted Domains, Send Connectors, etc., manually using the Exchange Management Console. An easier way is to use a synchronization process which synchronizes information from the Hub Transport Server within the company's Active Directory and Exchange organization to the Edge Transport Server in the DMZ. This process is called the Edge Transport Synchronization, or Edgesync.

2.6.3 Configuring Edge Transport Synchronization

As I mentioned, the Exchange Server 2010 Edge Transport Server is not part of the internal Active Directory and Exchange organization, and is typically installed in the network's DMZ. A mechanism obviously needs to be in place for keeping the server up to date with information.

For example, for the recipient filtering in the Edge Transport Server to take place, the server needs to know which recipients exist in the internal Exchange environment. The Edge Transport Server *also* needs to have knowledge about the existing Hub Transport Server in the internal Exchange organization, where the Edge Transport Server has to deliver its SMTP messages to.

This information is pushed from an internal Hub Transport Server to the Edge Transport Server by a process called Edgesync. Please note that for a successful synchronization from the Hub Transport Server to the Edge Transport Server, you have to open port 50636 on the internal firewall. This port has to be opened from the internal network to the DMZ and *not* vice versa.

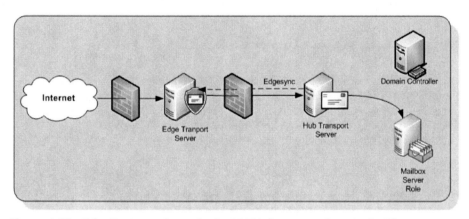

Figure 16: The Edge Transport Server in the DMZ is kept up to date via the Edgesync process.

To setup an Edge Synchronization, a special XML file has to be created on the Edge Transport Server. This XML file has to be imported to a Hub Transport Server on the internal network creating a relationship between the Edge Transport Server and the respective Hub Transport Server. Once that relationship is created, the Edgesync service can be started. To setup the Edgesync service, please follow these steps:

1. Log on to the Edge Transport Server using an administrator account and open an Exchange Management Shell.

2. Enter the following command:

```
New-EdgeSubscription -Filename <<filename.xml>>
```

Copy the <<filename.xml>> to a directory on the Hub Transport Server.

3. Log on to the Hub Transport Server using an administrator account and open an Exchange Management Shell command prompt.

4. Enter the following command:

```
New-EdgeSubscription -Filename <<filename.xml>> -CreateInternetSe
ndConnector:$TRUE -Site "Default-First-Site-Name"
```

When successfully finished on the Exchange Management Shell command prompt, enter the following command:

```
Start-EdgeSynchronization
```

The Edge Synchronization process should now successfully start.

5. On the Edge Transport Server, open the Exchange Management Shell and check if the settings are identical to the settings on the Hub Transport Server.

When making changes to the internal Exchange organization, these changes will automatically replicate to the Edge Transport Server in the DMZ.

2.7 Post-setup configuration

When the installations of both the internal Exchange organization and the Edge Transport Server are finished, the "post setup" configuration can be started. As in Exchange Server 2007, there are a couple of additions and changes in the configuration that have to be made to the Exchange Server 2010 instance before mail can be sent or received from the Internet:

*   Enter an Exchange Server 2010 license key.

*   Enter accepted domains and setup email address policies.

*   Configure a Send Connector to send email to the Internet.

*   Configure the Hub Transport Server to accept anonymous SMTP if an Edge Transport Server is not used.

*   Add a Certificate to the Client Access Server role.

*   Configure the Client Access Server role.

2.7.1 Exchange Server 2010 license key

The public Exchange Server 2010 Release Candidate does not need a license key, but the version that's available from the Microsoft download site at the time of writing has a lifetime of 120 days. Entering a license key is not possible in this Release Candidate version, but this will obviously change when Exchange Server 2010 gets to the Release To Manufacturing (RTM) stage.

2.7.2 Accepted domains

The first thing for Exchange Server 2010 to configure is the accepted domains. In order to receive SMTP messages from the Internet, an Exchange server has to know what domains it will be receiving email *for,* as well as which domains it is responsible for. These are called "accepted domains," and there are three types:

- **Authoritative Domain** – For this type of domain, the Exchange organization is fully responsible and there will be no other messaging environment responsible. This Exchange organization will also generate NDR (Non Delivery Report) messages when mailboxes are not available.

- **Internal Relay Domain** – The Exchange organization will receive mail for this type of domain, but it will relay all messages to an Exchange organization within the company.

- **External Relay Domain** – For this type of domain, the Exchange organization will receive mail, but it will relay all messages to a messaging platform outside the company.

For *all three* scenarios the MX records for the domain will be pointing to your Exchange organization, and mail will be initially delivered to your Exchange servers.

Accepted domains are configured on the organization level and, as such, are known by all Hub Transport Servers. If you are using an Edge Transport Server as well, the accepted domain information will also be synchronized to the Edge Transport Servers.

To configure accepted domains follow these steps:

1. Log on to an Exchange Server 2010 server with domain administrator credentials and open the Exchange Management Console.

2. Expand the "Microsoft Exchange On-Premises."

3. Expand the Organization Configuration.

4. Click on Hub Transport in the left pane.

5. In the middle pane there are eight tabs; click on the Accepted Domains one.

6. One entry will appear, and the name will be the local domain (FQDN) that's used when installing the Active Directory. In the Actions pane click on New Accepted Domain.

7. In the New Accepted Domain Wizard enter a (friendly) name and the Accepted Domain itself, for example *yourdomain.com*. When entered, select the type of Accepted Domain in your Exchange Organization. In this example select the "Authoritative Domain." Click New to continue.

8. The Accepted Domain will now be created, and you can now click Finish on the Completion window.

You have just created an accepted domain in your Exchange organization; the Exchange server will accept messages for this domain and, if no recipients are found, a NDR (Non Delivery Report) will be generated.

2.7.3 Email Address Policies

Exchange recipients clearly need an email address for receiving email. For receiving email from the Internet, recipients need an email address that corresponds to an accepted domain. Recipients are either assigned an email address using an Email Address Policy, or it is also possible to manually assign email addresses to recipients.

To configure Email Address Policies follow these steps:

1. Log on to an Exchange Server 2010 server with domain administrator credentials and open the Exchange Management Console.

2. Expand the "Microsoft Exchange On-Premises."

3. Expand the Organization Configuration.

4. Click on Hub Transport in the left pane.

5. In the middle pane there are eight tabs; click on the one labeled "Email Address Policies."

6. There will be one default policy that will be applied to all recipients in your organization. For now the default policy will be changed so that recipients will have the email address corresponding to your Accepted Domain. Click on "New Email Address Policy" to create a new policy.

7.   On the Introduction page enter a new friendly name. Click the Browse button to select a container or Organizational Unit in Active Directory where you want to apply the filter. Select the Users container. Click Next to continue.

8.   On the Conditions page you can select conditions on how the recipients in the container will be queried, for example on State, Province, Department, Company, etc. Do not select anything for this demonstration, and click Next to continue.

9.   On the Email Addresses tab click the Add button, the SMTP Email Address pop-up will be shown. Leave the local part default (Use Alias) and select the "Select the accepted domain for the email address" option and click Browse.

10. Select the Accepted Domain you entered earlier (in Section 2.7.2), click OK twice and click Next to continue.

11. On the Schedule page you have the option to apply the policy immediately or schedule a deploy during, for example, non-office hours. This is useful when you have to change thousands of recipients. For now leave it on Immediately and click Next to continue.

12. Review the settings and, if everything is OK, then click New to create the policy and apply it immediately.

13. When finished successfully, click the Finish button.

You can check the email address on a recipient through the EMC to confirm your policy has been correctly applied. Expand the Recipient Configuration in the left pane of the Exchange Management Console and click on "Mailbox." In the middle pane a list of recipients should show up, although right after installation only an administrator mailbox should be visible. Double-click on the mailbox and select the Email Addresses tab. The *Administrator@ yourdomain.com* should be the primary SMTP address.

2.7.4 Configure a Send Connector to the Internet

Exchange Server 2010 cannot send out SMTP messages to the Internet by default. To achieve this you'll need to create an SMTP connector, which is a connector between one or more Hub Transport Servers and the Internet. Since this information is stored in Active Directory, all Hub Transport Servers in the organization know of its existence and know how to route messages via the SMTP connector to the Internet.

To create an SMTP connector to the Internet, follow these steps:

1.   Log on to the Exchange Server 2010 server using a domain administrator account, and open the Exchange Management Console.

2. Expand "Microsoft Exchange On-Premises" and then expand the Organization Configuration.

3. Click on the Hub Transport, and then click on the "Send Connectors" tab in the middle pane.

4. In the Actions Pane click on "New Send Connector."

5. On the Introduction page enter a friendly name, "Internet Connector" for example, and in the "Select the intended use for this Send connector" drop-down box select the Internet option. Click Next to continue.

6. On the Address Space page, click on the Add button to add an address space for the Internet Connector. In the address field enter an asterisk *, leave the cost on default and click OK. Click Next to continue.

7. On the Network settings page you can select if the Send Connector will use its own network DNS settings to route email to other organizations, or to use a smart host. Change this according to your own environment and click Next to continue.

8. On the source server page you can choose multiple source servers for the Send Connector. You can compare this to Bridgehead Servers in Exchange Server 2003. When you enter multiple Hub Transport Servers, the Exchange organization will automatically load balance the SMTP traffic between the Hub Transport Servers. Since we have only one Hub Transport Server installed we can leave this as default. Click Next to continue.

9. Check the Configuration Summary, and if everything is OK click on New to create the Send Connector.

10. On the Completion page click Finish.

You have now created a Send Connector that routes messages from the internal Exchange Server 2010 organization to the Internet.

2.7.5 Add a certificate to the Client Access Server role

When the Exchange Server 2010 Client Access Server role is installed, a self-signed certificate is installed automatically, primarily for testing purposes. However, as soon as the installation is finished, a real certificate should be acquired and installed. Exchange Server 2010 uses a Unified Messaging certificate, which holds besides its Subject Name other names as well, called the Subject Alternative Names (SAN). For example, the Subject Name could be *webmail.yourdomain.com* and Subject Alternative Names could be *autodiscover.yourdomain.com* and *mail.yourdomain.com.*

To request a certificate you can either use the Exchange Management Console or the Exchange Management Shell. When using the Exchange Management Console (after all, we are Windows administrators, right?) use the following steps:

1. Log on to the Exchange Server 2010 Client Access Server and open the Exchange Management Console.

2. In the navigation pane, expand "Microsoft Exchange On-Premises."

3. In the navigation pane, click on "Server Configuration."

4. In the top half of the middle pane you'll see your Exchange Server, including your Edge Transport Server, and in the bottom half you'll see the corresponding certificate. This is the self-signed certificate that's created during the installation of your Exchange server.

5. In the actions pane click on "New Exchange Certificate," and the New Exchange Certificate wizard is shown. Enter a Friendly Name, for example "Exchange Server". Click Next to continue.

6. The next page is the Exchange Configuration where you can determine the usage of the certificate. Select the following services:

    • Client Access Server (Outlook Live)

    • Client Access Server (Exchange ActiveSync)

    • Client Access Server (Web Services, Outlook Anywhere and Autodiscover).

7. In all three options, enter the external hostname for your organization. In the last option also select "Autodiscover used on the Internet" and select the proper URL. The default is the Long URL like *autodiscover.yourdomain.com*. Click Next to continue.

8. In the Organization and Location page you have to enter your company specific details like Organization, Organizational Unit, Country, etc. In the Certificate Request File Path click Browse to enter a location for the Certificate Request File. Enter a filename like c:\ Exch-Cert.req and click Save. Click Next to continue.

9. On the Certificate Configuration page check your certificate request details and, if all is OK, click New to generate the request file.

10. On the completion page you'll see the PowerShell command that was used for generating this certificate request. If needed you can use CTRL-C to copy the contents of this page to the server's clipboard. Click Finish to continue.

You can find the file c:\Exch-Cert.req on your server. This file looks something like this:

```
-----BEGIN NEW CERTIFICATE REQUEST-----
MIIETjCCAzYCAQAwfTEcMBoGA1UEAwwTd2VibWFpbC5pbmZyYW1hbi5ubDEPMA0G
A1UECwwGT2ZmaWN1MRcwFQYDVQQKDA5ETS1Db25zdWx0aW50czESMBAGA1UEBwwJ
RW1tZWxvb3JkMRIwEAYDVQQIDAlGbGV2b2xhbmQxCzAJBgNVBAYTAk5MMIIBIjAN
BgkqhkiG9w0BAQEFAAOCAQ8AMIIBCgKCAQEA+GeyjN42E74rjnuqG7BCv8K1BHrO
P6bgsJchLZcHj0IvdnCTPtXpd1GuGWLWf1F3AQNZ2inen8xBhZrkjCkcdBGyVbyz
z/kDzaJMQA2B+qzJ0uKJA2J8zYj9Krzh5tgTF4sqDtt10jRNLxsdEIFTcj3gCdvL
jUI86RQdonQ49OkJ2E89BYXGoI+Py06/jGx5Oc7zoEiONQFfV7uqFIvGUrd75uwL
Yha8pXQLhVBTgm74yhwI3pF8FuOF/38mUyoL8HgHuzbSYBgquQxpQXcSqEJt0uHg
fhIuzj4jv80eJdm83g15nxpK/cXWIgYYVsJ71Ij2Qpsensek6A17mYULHQIDAQAB
oIIBijAaBgorBgEEAYI3DQIDMQwWCjYuMS43NjAwLjIwVwYJKwYBBAGCNxUUMUow
SAIBBQwRVF1QMjAxMC5FMTQuTE9DQUWwMDEUxNFxUWVAyMDEwJAwiTW1jm9zb2Z0
LkV4Y2hhbmd1LlNlcnZpY2VIb3N0LLmV4ZTByBgorBgEEAYI3DQICMWQwYgIBAR5a
AE0AaQBjAHIAbwBzAG8AZgB0ACAAUgBTAEEAIABTAEMAaABhAG4AbgBlAGwAIABD
AHIAeQBwAHQAbwBnAHIAYQBwAGgAaAQBjACAAUAByAG8AdgBpAGQAZQByAwEAMIGe
BgkqhkiG9w0BCQ4xgZAwgY0wDgYDVR0PAQH/BAQDAgWgME4GA1UdEQRHMEWCE3d1
Ym1haWwuaW5mcmFtFtYW4ubmnycCEGlhaWwuaW5mcmFtYW4ubmycCFUUyMDEwRnVsbC5F
MjAxMC5sb2NhbIIFRTIwMTAwDAYDVR0TAQH/BAIwADAdBgNVHQ4EFgQUAHF6b9FN
/hPwzjNQ8HcaczrsGlowDQYJKoZIhvcNAQEFBQADggEBANDo8kMo/1psGWInI9vg
zFKsZqRGkpnYE+Uhhy0S3BSnUQTY4c+ulP5DgXLi0814i6mzjROSPrUJUZOSqY2E
nIinTDj4QbBRgwPKIT/9Fh6sbvN3PjTWfDON8GO21PEy3ffeA30+SkaKJ6h2AnDO
OXFv5p03zjAC3R2M31kDB6os3E+vBJt+dxwdXLFrgLTjceFj1yhb7cTKPwDRq4wU
2uMMtDmaOhN8w3t/00m9fwklJp5zz1RY1+AD19sXAzeXOzrgWmJu9HDw0YqgDVRs
SdqEoMulw7mvumMwF7PQYGqp6w7m/6k9OwgcR1Mr7Mc3RZV25xcTawRfVFDw3BEk
80Y=
-----END NEW CERTIFICATE REQUEST-----
```

To request a new certificate, you have to submit this file to your Certificate Authority. Microsoft has a list on their support website of supported vendors who can supply Unified Communications certificates: HTTP://TINYURL.COM/CERTVENDORS.

On the Exchange Certificates tab in the Exchange Management Console, you'll see a new entry, and the parameters you entered in the previous step can be identified here.

When you receive the certificate from your authority follow these steps:

1. Save the certificate on the hard disk of your server.

2. In the Exchange Management Console, on the Exchange Certificates tab, right-click the new certificate and select "Complete Pending Request."

3. Browse to the file you stored in Step 1 on the hard disk.

4. Follow the wizard to complete the certificate request and finish the installation.

5. In the Exchange Management Console, on the Exchange Certificates tab select the original, self-signed certificate, right-click it, and select Remove to remove this certificate from the Exchange Server 2010 server.

6. Using Internet Explorer open Outlook Web App (using HTTPS://LOCALHOST/OWA) and check the new certificate. Never mind the error message you will receive, this is because the name "localhost" is not in the certificate.

You can also use the Exchange Management Shell to request a new certificate:

7. Log on to the Exchange Server 2010 server with domain administrator credentials and open the Exchange Management Shell.

8. Since the –Path option is no longer supported in Exchange Server 2010 you first have to use a variable and in Step 2 you have to write the actual file:

```
$CertData = New-ExchangeCertificate -FriendlyName 'Exchange
Server' -GenerateRequest -PrivateKeyExportable:$TRUE
-DomainName:webmail.inframan.nl, mail.inframan.nl,E2010Full.
E2010.local,E2010
-SubjectName "C=NL,S=Flevoland,L=Emmeloord,O=DM-
Consultants,OU=Office, CN=webmail.inframan.nl"

Set-Content -Path c:\cert-req.txt -Value $CertData
This command will generate a certificate request file identical
to the request you created in the GUI and that can be submitted
at your own certificate authority.
```

A certificate will be sent by your certificate authority that can be imported on the Client Access Server by using the Import-ExchangeCertificate commandlet in the Exchange Management Shell. The output of this commandlet can be piped into the Enable-ExchangeCertificate to enable the certificate after importing it:

1. Log on to the Exchange Server 2010 server with domain administrator credentials and open the Exchange Management Shell.

2. Enter the following command:

```
Import-ExchangeCertificate -FileData ($(Get-Content -Path c:\
cert-new.cer -Encoding byte)) | Enable-ExchangeCertificate-
Services POP,IMAP,IIS,SMTP
2.7.6        Configure the Client Access Server role
```

The Client Access Server role is responsible for handling all client requests with respect to mailbox access. This means Outlook Web App, POP3 and IMAP4, Outlook Anywhere and ActiveSync all have to be configured on the Client Access Server role. New in Exchange Server 2010 is the fact that the Client Access Server now also handles all MAPI requests. So Outlook clients no longer connect to the Mailbox Server role directory, but rather to the Client Access Server. This functionality is called "RPC Client Access." The codename for this was "MAPI on the Middle Tier" or MoMT.

In this section, I will briefly focus on Outlook Web App, Outlook Anywhere and ActiveSync. A prerequisite for proper functioning of these services is that a valid Unified Communications certificate from a trusted vendor, with proper Subject Alternative Names is installed as described in Section 2.7.5. Since the Client Access Server is on the same box as the Mailbox Server, no special configuration is needed for the MAPI clients.

1. Log on to the Exchange Server 2010 server with domain administrator credentials and open the Exchange Management Console.

2. In the navigation pane expand "Microsoft Exchange On-Premises."

3. In the navigation pane expand "Server Configuration."

4. Click on "Client Access."

5. In the lower part of the results pane you can select the tabs for Outlook Web App, Exchange ActiveSync, Offline Address Book Distribution and POP3 and IMAP4. From here, you can now configure the various aspects of the Client Access Server.

Outlook Web App

1. To configure Outlook Web App select the Outlook Web App tab, right-click on OWA (Default Website) and select its properties.

2. In the External URL field, enter the URL that users will use when connecting to the OWA site from the Internet. Make sure that this name corresponds to the name used in the certificate you installed in the previous section.

3. Click OK to close the properties page.

Exchange ActiveSync

1. On the Exchange ActiveSync tab, right-click the Microsoft-Server-ActiveSync and select its properties.

2. In the External URL field, enter the URL that users will use when connecting to the OWA site from the internet. Make sure that this name corresponds to the name used in the certificate you installed in the previous section.

3. Click OK to close the properties page.

Note

Testing your Exchange Server 2010 ActiveSync setup is always difficult. To avoid needing a real mobile device you can use an emulator for testing purposes. Microsoft has several emulators available on the Microsoft download site, and you can download the Windows Mobile 6.5 emulator here: HTTP://TINYURL.COM/WINMOB6. Just install it on your computer or laptop, connect it to your local network adapter and start configuring the device. When you have the proper connectivity you can even test it from home – this works great!

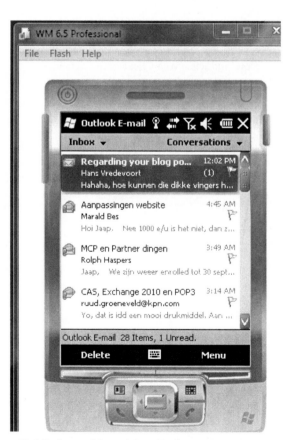

Figure 17: Windows Mobile 6.5 working with an Exchange Server 2010.

Outlook Anywhere

Outlook Anywhere uses the HTTP protocol to encapsulate RPC information for sending between the Outlook client (version 2003 and 2007) and the Exchange Server 2010 server. For this service to run properly the RPC over HTTP Proxy service has to be installed on the Client Access Server. This can be achieved either by adding this as a feature via the Server Manager, or by entering the following command on a PowerShell Command Prompt:

```
ServerManagerCmd.exe -i RPC-over-HTTP-proxy
When the RPC over HTTP Proxy is installed use the following steps
to configure Outlook Anywhere:
```

1.   Open the Exchange Management Console.

2.   In the navigation pane, expand "Microsoft Exchange On-Premises."

3.   In the navigation pane, expand "Server Configuration."

4.   Click on "Client Access" and select your Client Access Server.

5.   In the Actions pane, click on "Enable Outlook Anywhere."

6.   On the Enable Outlook Anywhere page enter the External host name. Make sure that this name is also available in the certificate you created on the previous Paragraph. Select the authentication methods used by clients, i.e. Basic Authentication or NTLM authentication. For now leave these settings on default and click Enable to continue.

7.   This will activate the Outlook Anywhere service on this service, and it may take up to 15 minutes before the service is actually usable on the Client Access Server. Click Finish to close the wizard.

2.8 Summary

Installing Exchange Server 2010 is really quite easy. There are a number of prerequisites, like the .NET Framework 3.5 and PowerShell Version 2, which should all be running on Windows Server 2008 or Windows Server 2008 R2. Looking at the prerequisites that need to be installed on Windows Server 2008, which are available out of the box in Windows Server 2008 R2, in my humble opinion it's a no-brainer to not use Windows Server 2008 at all. Although Exchange Server 2010 is not supported on Windows Server 2003, the Active Directory can be running on Windows Server 2003, as long as the servers are on a Service Pack 1 level.

Compared to Exchange Server 2007, Microsoft made quite a number of improvements to the Exchange Management Console, *especially* when it comes to certificates. This has always been a serious pain for most Exchange Administrators in the past. They've done a good job of streamlining that process, and taking a lot of the headache out of it.

This chapter described a fresh installation of Exchange Server 2010, which I guess will not happen too often in the real world. The next chapter deals with some coexistence scenarios, i.e. installation of Exchange Server 2010 into an existing Exchange Server 2003 or Exchange Server 2007 environment. This will probably be by far the more common situation SysAdmins will find themselves in, although I will be referring back to this chapter when discussing the basic installation steps.

Chapter 3: Exchange Server 2010 Coexistence

As we've seen, installing Exchange Server 2010 in a greenfield situation and configuring it correctly isn't that difficult. However, there is a distinct possibility that you already have an Exchange organization deployed, be it Exchange Server 2007 or Exchange Server 2003.

In fact, a large proportion of Exchange Server customers in the last few years have decided that they are *not* going to upgrade from their existing Exchange Server 2003 infrastructure to a new Exchange Server 2007 one. A commonly heard reason for this is that 2003 "is good enough." To be fair, if the scalability, Unified Messaging or High Availability options in Exchange Server 2007 don't offer you a solid business case for upgrading, this decision is perfectly understandable.

But with Exchange Server 2010 things will change. Besides all of the new functionality, if you are still running Exchange Server 2003, you'll find that Microsoft will deprecate the support on Exchange Server 2003. The support on Exchange Server 2003 will not stop immediately, but Microsoft's focus will be on Exchange Server 2010 and Exchange Server 2007. So, if you want to make sure you're fully supported, upgrading to Exchange Server 2010 can be done in two ways:

* **Integrate Exchange Server 2010 into your existing Exchange infrastructure and transition your mailboxes to the new Exchange servers**.
  This method can be done when you are running on Exchange Server 2007 or Exchange Server 2003.

* **Build a new Active Directory and a new Exchange Server 2010 organization and migrate your mailboxes to the new environment**.
  This is the preferred method if your current environment is not compatible with Exchange Server 2010.

I've chosen my terminology carefully here, so as to be consistent with other documentation you may encounter. Moving mailboxes from Exchange Server 2003 to Exchange Server 2010 in one organization is called *transitioning*. If Exchange Server 2010 is installed in a new Active Directory forest and mailboxes are moved from one Active Directory forest to another it's called a *migration*.

This chapter will focus on integrating Exchange Server 2010 into an existing Exchange Server 2003 or Exchange Server 2007 environment (the first method), but bear in mind that Exchange Server 2010 **cannot** be installed into an existing Exchange Server 2000 environment. This is enforced in the Exchange setup programs, which will check on the current version of all Exchange servers. If Exchange Server 2000 is detected on *any* server, the setup program will display an error and abort.

Exchange Server 2010 *does* support the following scenarios:

*   Single Forest, Single Active Directory site.

*   Single Forest, Multiple Active Directory sites.

*   Multiple Forest, Multiple Active Directory sites.

*   Coexistence with Exchange Server 2003 SP2. Older versions of Exchange Server are not supported in an Exchange Server 2010 coexistence scenario.

*   Coexistence with Exchange Server 2007 SP2. Older versions of Exchange Server 2007 are not supported in an Exchange Server 2010 coexistence scenario.

Note

When transitioning to Exchange Server 2010, you must start with the Internet-facing Active Directory site. Other Active Directory sites will be moved later on in the transition process. Starting with internal Active Directory sites is not supported.

The rest of this chapter is split into two sections, each of which will aim to get you running Exchange Server 2010 in coexistence with the respective older environments.
In each section, I'll cover:

*   The order in which the different servers should be installed.

*   Active Directory upgrades and prerequisite considerations.

*   The actual installation process for Exchange Server 2010.

*   The SMTP infrastructure.

*   Moving mailboxes.

You'll notice a certain amount of replication between the two sections (if you read them both), but I've tried to minimize that by referring to instructions where possible, rather than duplicating them. In any case, you should be able to pick the section most relevant to you and find everything you need to get you started.

3.1 Coexistence with Exchange Server 2003

You won't be too surprised to hear that there are a *lot* of differences between Exchange Server 2003 and Exchange Server 2010. The most important are:

*   Exchange Server 2010 is available only in a 64-bit version.

*   Exchange Server 2010 does not use Administrative Groups for delegation of control.

*   Exchange Server 2010 does not use Routing Groups for routing messages.

*   Exchange Server 2010 does not use Link State Routing for updating the routing table.

*   Exchange Server 2010 does not use the Recipient Update Service for setting Exchange properties on recipient objects.

This is a much more extensive list than the differences with Exchange Server 2007, and the differences themselves are also more significant. Just to make sure everyone is on the same proverbial page as I go through this, I'll lay down a little background information on each of these legacy systems (e.g. Administrative Groups) before I explain what's changed.

3.1.1 64-bit support

Exchange Server 2010 is only available in a 64-bit version, as the Exchange Product Group at Microsoft is taking full advantage of the hardware advances since Exchange Server 2007 was released. The current 32-bit (X86) platform was developed in the mid-eighties, and has a 4 GB memory limit. In those days, 4 GB of memory was beyond everyone's imagination. Today, 4 GB of memory is commonly installed in a laptop.

As the successor of the 32-bit platform, one of the clear advantages of 64-bit is a theoretical memory limit of 2^{64} bytes, or 16 PB (Petabytes). Windows obviously cannot address this amount of memory at this time, but the current memory limit of Windows Server 2008 R2 Enterprise is 2 TB (Terabytes). Naturally, current processors just cannot address anything like that much physical memory, but Moore's law and the inexorable march of technological progress mean that this limit will keep being pushed back in the future.

Whilst 4 GB of memory might be enough for a laptop or workstation, for large server applications like Exchange server, a mere 4 GB of memory is a huge limitation. A fact which can be clearly illustrated in Exchange Server 2003, when having more than 2,000 mailboxes on one Exchange server will result in a severe disk I/O penalty, which typically results in an expensive storage solution.

There are special techniques for addressing more than 4 GB of memory on the 32-bit platform, like Physical Address Extensions (PAE), which you can read more about here:

HTTP://TINYURL.COM/32BITPAE

However, Exchange Server 2003 does not use this technique, and so is stuck with the 4 GB memory limit (and you can read more about that here: HTTP://TINYURL.COM/2003LIMIT). Given that Exchange server 2010 is 64-bit only, this automatically implies that an in-place upgrade of Exchange Server 2003 server to Exchange Server 2010 is impossible. *A new Exchange Server 2010 server in a 2003 environment always needs to be installed on separate hardware.* I'll mention briefly now that the same is true for Exchange Server 2007; although it is also a 64-bit application, Microsoft does not support an in-place upgrade due to technical complexity in both products.

3.1.2 Administrative Groups are no longer used for delegation of control

Exchange Server 2003 uses Administrative Groups for delegation of control, allowing you to create multiple Administrative Groups and delegate control of them to different administrators. For example, a large multinational company could create multiple Administrative Groups, one for each country, and each country could have its own Exchange administration department, responsible for maintaining their local Exchange servers. This could be achieved by delegating control of the appropriate Administrative Group to *specific* Universal Security Groups, which these Exchange administrators are, in turn, assigned to. This sounds pretty complicated, and after seeing such a scenario in real life, I can assure you that it *is* complicated. And besides being complicated, it is prone to error and I've seen it bring a world-wide deployment to its knees. It's a good thing Microsoft is not continuing this path!

Exchange Server 2010 does not use Administrative Groups any more. During installation of the *first* Exchange Server 2010 server, a new Administrative Group will be created in Active Directory, called *"Exchange Administrative Group (FYDIBOHF23SPDLT)."* All subsequent servers will be installed in this Administrative Group. Delegation of control in Exchange Server 2010 is achieved by implementing a Role Based Access (RBAC) model. To be honest, this won't really affect the installation process, so I will explain the RBAC model in more detail in Chapter 4.

3.1.3 Routing Groups are no longer used for routing messages

For routing messages between different locations, Exchange Server 2003 uses a concept called Routing Groups. A Routing Group can be identified as a location with a high bandwidth and low latency network, such as an office with a 100 Mbps internal network where all Exchange Server 2003 servers have full access to each other all the time. When multiple locations are present, each has their own Routing Group, and each Routing Group is connected with each other using "slow links." These Routing Groups in an Exchange organization are connected using Routing Group Connectors, and so Routing Groups are very similar to Sites in Active Directory. Active Directory sites have already existed since Windows 2000 Active Directory, but Exchange Server 2003 just didn't use them and relied on their own mechanism. And to be honest, this really didn't make sense.

Instead of Routing Groups, Exchange Server 2010 now uses Active Directory sites to route messages to Exchange servers in other locations. To connect Exchange Server 2010 with an Exchange Server 2003 environment in the same Active Directory forest (and thus the same Exchange organization), a special Routing Group, called "*Exchange Routing Group (DWBGZMFD01QNBJR)*" will be created during the installation of the first Exchange Server 2010 server. A special Interop Routing Group Connector will also be created during the setup of that initial server, in order to route messages between Exchange Server 2003 and Exchange Server 2010.

It's also worth bearing in mind that since Exchange Server 2010 uses Active Directory sites for routing SMTP messages, every site that contains an Exchange Server 2010 Mailbox Server role will also need an Exchange Server 2010 Hub Transport Server role to be installed.

3.1.4 Link State Routing is no longer used for updating the routing table

To keep routing information up to date in Exchange Server 2003, a process called *Link State* is used. When a connector in Exchange Server 2003 changes its state, the Routing Table used by the Routing Group connectors is updated, and this Routing Table is sent immediately to other Exchange servers in the same Routing Group. When an Exchange Server 2003 server initiates an SMTP connection to a similar server in another Routing Group, the Routing Tables on both servers are compared and, if needed, the newer version of the Routing Table is sent to the other server.

This works fine as long as the Routing Table is not very large, but there are known cases, with over 75 Routing Groups and hundreds of Routing Group Connectors, where the Routing Table was between 750KB and 1MB in size. It might not sound like much, but when a Routing

Table is being exchanged frequently, this will have a noticeable negative impact on the network traffic across the WAN.

Note

More information regarding message routing in Exchange Server 2003 can be found in the "Exchange Server Transport and Routing Guide" which is on the Microsoft TechNet site: HTTP://TINYURL.COM/ROUTINGGUIDE. *When you want to take a closer look at the routing table in your own Exchange Server 2003 environment, you can download the WinRoute tool from the Microsoft website:* HTTP://TINYURL.COM/WINROUTE.

Exchange Server 2010 has replaced this whole system with Active Directory Site Links (as explained above) and thus leverages Active Directory information to determine an alternate route when a specific link is no longer available. Before installing the first Exchange Server 2010 server into an existing Exchange Server 2003 environment, Link State Updates *need* to be suppressed to avoid routing conflicts between the Exchange versions.

3.1.5 Recipient Update Service versus Email Address Policies

The Recipient Update Service (RUS) in Exchange Server 2003 is the service that is responsible for updating the Exchange specific properties of Exchange recipients in Active Directory. When a user is created with Active Directory Users and Computers, the RUS will pick up the user account and "stamp" it with Exchange-specific attributes, such as the homeserver, homeMTA, homeMDB and email addresses. It can take some time for a user to be fully provisioned and available, especially on busy servers. The Service is part of the System Attendant, and only one instance is running in each Active Directory domain.

Exchange Server 2010 does not use the Recipient Update Service anymore, but uses Email Address Policies instead. When a mailbox-enabled user is created, an Email Address Policy is applied immediately, and the mailbox is therefore available instantly, though of course the user object needs to be replicated between all Domain Controllers in your environment to be fully available at all locations. In a coexistence scenario, the Recipient Update Service and the accompanying Recipient Policies can only be managed from the Exchange Server 2003 System Manager, and the Exchange Server 2010 Address List Policies can only be managed from the Exchange Management Console or the Exchange Management Shell. The only time a Recipient Policy is accessed using the Exchange Management Shell is when upgrading the Recipient Policy to an Email Address Policy.

3.2 Installing Exchange Server 2010 in an Exchange Server 2003 environment

Before installing the first Exchange Server 2010 server into an existing Exchange Server 2003 environment, a number of prerequisites have to be met:

- All domains in the existing Active Directory forest containing Exchange Recipients have to be running in *native mode*.

- The Active Directory forest has to be running on a *Windows Server 2003 forest functionality level.*

- Each site in Active Directory should have at least one Domain Controller, and the Global Catalog server needs to be on a *Windows Server 2003 SP2 level*. Although not required, it is recommended to have 64-bit type Domain Controllers and Global Catalog Servers for best performance.

- The Schema Master of the Active Directory needs to be a *Windows Server 2003 SP2* or *Windows Server 2008 server*. This can be either a 64-bit or an 32-bit server.

- *All* Exchange 2003 servers must have *Service Pack 2* installed.

In addition to that, the server where Exchange Server will be installed also needs to meet the **following prerequisites**:

- The server needs to be a *64-bit* computer.

- *Windows Server 2008 SP2* or *Windows Server 2008 R2 64-bit* needs to be installed.

- *Internet Information Server* needs to be installed.

- *Windows Remote Management (WinRM) 2.0* needs to be installed.

- *PowerShell 2.0* needs to be installed.

- *.NET Framework 3.5 SP1* needs to be installed.

Depending on the version of Windows 2008 you're using (i.e. Service Pack 2 or R2), a number of hotfixes will also need to be installed. I would strongly recommend that you bring your server up to date with the latest hotfixes from Microsoft Update, preferably before you perform this installation.

To make the process of installing prerequisites as painless as possible, the Exchange Server product group has created a series of XML files that can be used to automatically install Internet Information Server on your computer, together with the other prerequisites for Exchange Server 2010. These files are located on your installation media in the "scripts" directory.

To install the Internet Information Server (and other prerequisites) in a configuration needed to support, for example, an Exchange Server 2010 *Client Access Server*, you can use the "Exchange-CAS.xml" file with the following command:

```
ServerManagerCmd.exe -inputpath Exchange-CAS.xml
```

If you are using Windows Server 2008 R2, you will get a warning about ServerManagerCmd. exe being deprecated under Windows Server 2008 R2, but it still works fine – go ahead and run it.

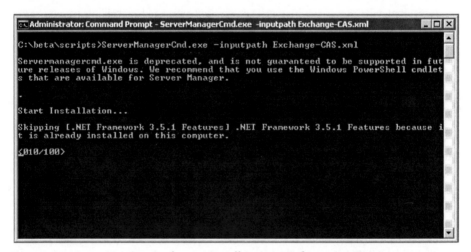

Figure 1: Use ServerManagerCmd.exe to install Internet Information Server.

3.2.1 Exchange Server 2010 order of installation

Although Exchange Server 2010 can be installed into an existing Exchange Server 2003 environment – in the same forest and the same domain – there are some issues with compatibility, and you have to take the installation order of the Exchange Server 2010 servers into account.

- **First** – Exchange Server 2010 *Client Access Server*. The Client Access Server can work with an Exchange Server 2003 Mailbox Server as well as an Exchange Server 2010 Mailbox Server.

- **Second** – Exchange Server 2010 *Hub Transport Server*. Between the Hub Transport Server and the Exchange 2003 (front-end) server, a so called "Interop Routing Group Connector" will be created to enable SMTP messages to be sent back and forth between the two environments.

- **Third** – Exchange Server 2010 *Mailbox Server role*. After you've installed the Mailbox Server role and established a proper Public Folder replication between Exchange Server 2003 and Exchange Server 2010, you can start moving mailboxes to the new Mailbox Server.

- **The Exchange Server 2010 Edge Transport Server role can be installed at any time during the upgrade, but the Edge Transport Server features are only fully available when the Exchange Server Hub Transport Server is installed.**

Note

An in-place upgrade to Exchange Server 2010 is NOT supported in any scenario!

3.2.2 Installing Exchange Server 2010

Although you will need to install each of the Exchange Server 2010 server roles in a specific order, these roles can of course be combined on one machine.

Installing Exchange Server 2010 into an existing Exchange Server 2003 environment is pretty straightforward. The process can be broken down into the following easy steps:

- Exchange Server readiness check (as part of the Best Practices Analyzer).

- Upgrading the Active Directory Schema.

- Upgrading the Exchange organization.

- Upgrading the Active Directory domain.

- Installing the first Exchange Server 2010 server.

When you start the GUI setup application of Exchange Server 2010 (setup.exe), all these steps will be performed automatically in the correct order. I'll go through them in more detail here because you can use the command-line version of setup if you want to fully control the options and execution of the setup program.

Note

The first step, running the Exchange Server Best Practices Analyzer readiness check, was not available during the beta timeframe of Exchange Server 2010. It will be made available in a future release.

3.2.2.1 Upgrading the Active Directory

The first step in changing your configuration for Exchange Server 2010 is upgrading the Active Directory schema to the Exchange Server 2010 level. You can achieve this by opening a command prompt on the Active Directory schema master from the Exchange Server 2007 installation media, and running the following commands:

```
Setup.com /PrepareLegacyExchangePermissions <<domainname>>


Setup.com /PrepareSchema
```

The first command, with /PrepareLegacyExchangePermissions, grants new permissions to ensure that the Recipient Update Service in Exchange Server 2003 continues to run correctly after the schema change to Exchange Server 2010 (which is performed in the next step). The **/PrepareLegacyExchangePermissions** must be performed before the actual upgrade of the Schema, which is what the *second* command does.

If you want to change the Schema on a computer that's not the Schema Master, you have to make sure that the LDIFDE application is available on that computer. You can install this by opening a command prompt and entering the following:

```
ServerManagerCmd.exe -I RSAT-ADDS
```

You can check what version your schema is, or check if the upgrade was successful, using a tool like ADSIEDIT or LDP.EXE and checking the *CN=ms-Exch-Schema-Version-Pt object* in the Active Directory schema. After the schema change, its "*rangeUpper*" property should have the value **14529** (or higher, as this value is for Beta1 of Exchange Server 2010 and will change with later versions). Just so you know, the property can have the following values:

Value	Corresponding Exchange version
6870	Exchange Server 2003 RTM
6936	Exchange Server 2003 service pack 2
10628	Exchange Server 2007
11116	Exchange Server 2007 service pack 1
14622	Exchange Server 2007 service pack 2
14622	Exchange Server 2010

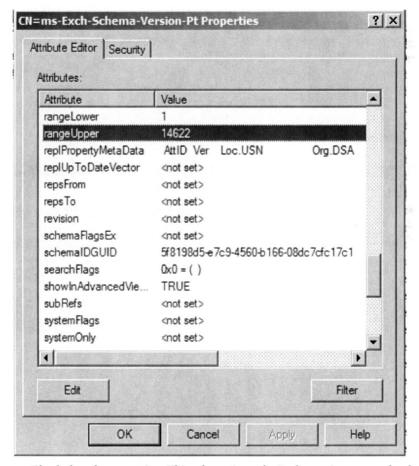

Figure 2: Check the schema version. This schema is on the Exchange Server 2010 level.

Note

If you have multiple domain controllers in your Exchange Server environment, you'll have to wait for the Domain Controller replication to finish before you continue to the next step.

After upgrading the Schema, the current Exchange Server 2003 organization can be upgraded to support Exchange Server 2010. To do this, run the following command from the Exchange Server 2010 installation media:

```
Setup.com /PrepareAD
```

This simple command automatically configures the global Exchange objects in Active Directory (residing in the Active Directory Configuration container), creates the Exchange Universal Security Groups in the root of the domain, and prepares the current domain for Exchange Server 2010.

It *also* creates the Exchange 2010 Administrative Group called "Exchange Administrative Group (FYDIBOHF23SPDLT)" and Exchange 2010 Routing Group called "Exchange Routing Group (DWBGZMFD01QNBJR)" if they didn't already exist (see Sections **3.1.2.** and **3.1.3** if you missed the significance of this).

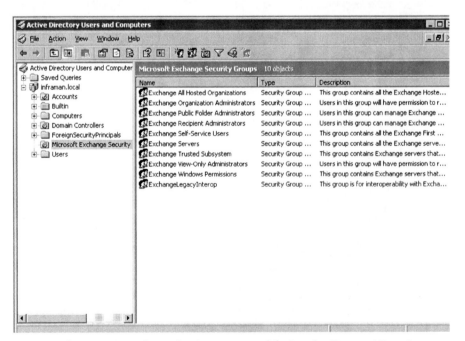

Figure 3: Exchange Universal Security Groups created during the /PrepareAD option.

To verify that this step completed successfully, make sure that there is a new organizational unit (OU) in the root domain called **Microsoft Exchange Security Groups** and that this container contains the groups shown in Figure 3.

After running the setup.com application with the **/PrepareAD** switch, the newly created Administrative Group will show up in the Exchange Server 2003 System Manager, as you can see in Figure 4.

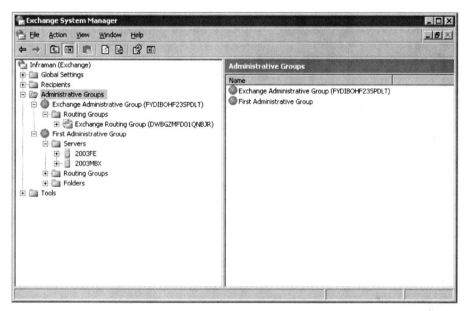

Figure 4: The Exchange Server 2010 Administrative Groups shows up after running setup. com /PrepareAD.

The last step in preparing your environment for the implementation of Exchange Server 2010 is to prepare the Active Directory domain (or domains) for Exchange Server 2010. The domain is prepared by running the following command from the Exchange Server 2010 installation media:

```
Setup.com /PrepareDomain
```

When you have multiple domains holding Exchange Recipients in your Active Directory forest, and you want to prepare all domains in one step you can replace the **/PrepareDomain** with **/PrepareAllDomains**.

This sets the necessary permissions on the Exchange Server container in Active Directory, as well as for the Exchange Servers, the Exchange Administrators and Authenticated Users. It also creates a new Global Group called "**Exchange domain servers**" in the domain where the command is run. This Global Group is only used for installing Exchange Server 2010 servers in a child domain, in a site other than the root domain. The setup program uses this to avoid installation issues when the Domain Controllers haven't yet fully replicated all the updated information.

After performing these easy steps, the Active Directory and Exchange Server environment is fully prepared for the installation of the first Exchange Server 2010 server!

3.2.2.2 Installing the first Exchange Server 2010 server

In our example Exchange Server 2003 environment, we will implement a combined Exchange Server 2010 Hub Transport and Client Access Server, and a dedicated Exchange Server 2010 Mailbox Server. Both the Client Access and Hub Transport Servers will need to have Internet Information Server installed.

To install a combined Exchange Server 2010 Hub Transport and Client Access Server into the nicely prepared Exchange Server 2003 environment, you can follow these steps:

1. Log on to the new server where you want to install Exchange Server 2010. Make sure that the server is a member of the domain where Exchange Server 2003 is installed, and that all the prerequisite software is installed.

2. Go to the installation media and start the *setup.exe* installation program. The setup splash screen appears and, if all prerequisite software is installed correctly, the first three steps are grayed out.

3. If needed, download the language files, or else just use the languages provided on the DVD. You have to select one of these options to proceed.

4. When you've finished downloading the language files, select "Step 5: Install Microsoft Exchange" and click Next to move past the Introduction page.

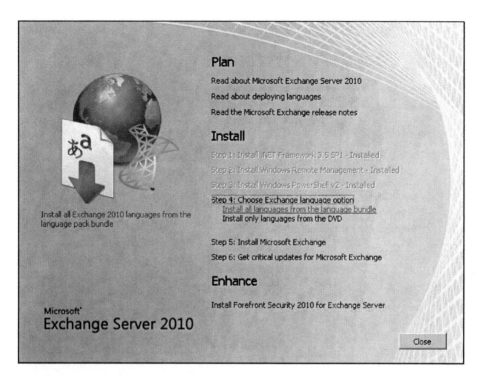

Figure 5: Choose Step 4 if you want to install non-English language packs.

5.   Accept the license agreement and click Next.

6.   If wanted, you can select the error reporting option. Click Next.

7.   In the "Installation Type" screen, you can choose between a Typical Installation or a Custom Installation, which is identical to the installation process in Chapter 2. Select Custom Exchange Server Installation and click Next.

8.   As we're only installing the Hub Transport Server and Client Access Server roles, you need to ensure that those are the only two options selected from the component list. The Exchange Management Tools will be automatically installed with any Exchange Server role.

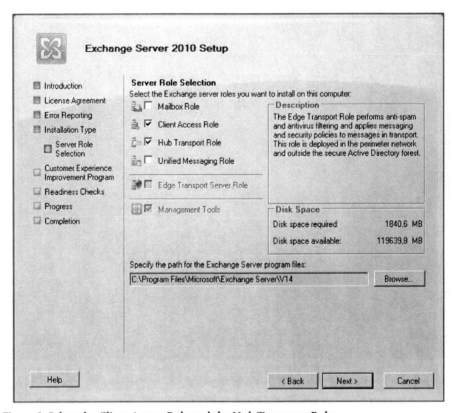

Figure 6: Select the Client Access Role and the Hub Transport Role.

Click Next to continue.

9. With the Exchange Server 2010 setup program, there's the option to configure the Client Access Server role as an Internet-facing server. If that's what you want, you can just tick the relevant checkbox and enter the domain name you want to use when accessing the Client Access Server from the Internet.

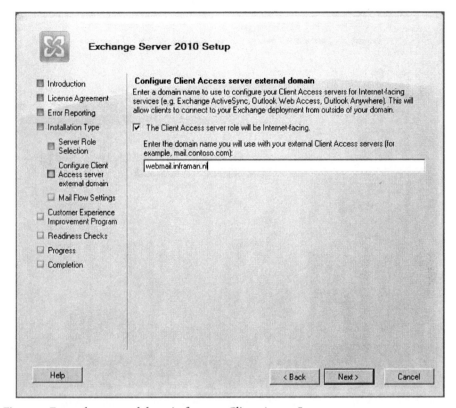

Figure 7: Enter the external domain for your Client Access Server.

10. It is also possible to leave this field blank and enter the parameters during the later configuration of the servers. For now we'll use this option, so enter your own domain name and click Next to continue;

11. The "*Mail Flow Settings*" screen will only appear when performing a transition from Exchange Server 2003 to Exchange Server 2010. Using the Browse button, you select which 2003 Exchange Server will be assigned as a hub server for an Interop Routing Group Connector, which both Exchange Server 2003 and Exchange Server 2010 use for sending messages to each other (see Section **3.1.3**).

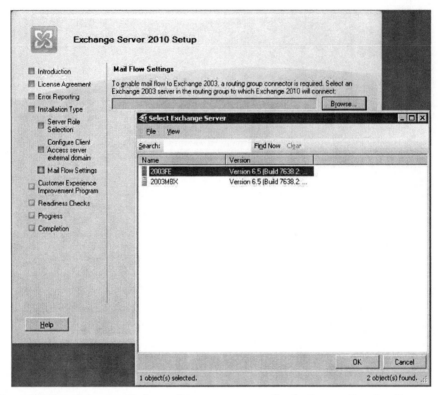

Figure 8: Select the proper Exchange Server 2003 server for the Interop Routing Group Connector.

12. In this example we'll select the 2003FE server, which is an Exchange Server 2003 Front-End server. Click OK and Next.

13. In the "Customer Experience Improvement Program" screen you can select whether or not you want to participate in this program. There's no trick to this, so you can just make your selection and click Next.

14. The setup application will now check the readiness of the Exchange configuration. If issues are found, they are presented at this stage and you'll have the opportunity to resolve them. If no issues are found, just click Install.

15. The Exchange Server 2010 server will now be installed. For every step a progress bar is shown.

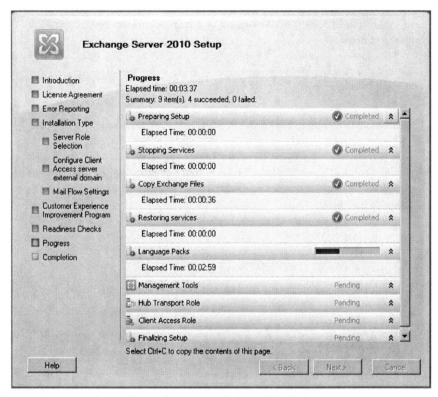

Figure 9: A progress bar is shown during installation of Exchange Server 2010.

16. When all steps are completed, click Finish, and then click "Close" on the Welcome screen to end the setup program. You can continue to check the installation using the Exchange Management Console, which is automatically opened after the setup.

3.2.2.3 Installing the Exchange Server 2010 Mailbox Server

As we've only installed a Client Access Server and Hub Transport Server, we still need to go through the installation process for an Exchange Server 2010 Mailbox Server. The steps are very similar, but there *are* some small differences.

1. Log on to the server that will hold the Mailbox Server role. Make sure that it is a member of the domain and that all prerequisite software is installed.

2. If you haven't done so already, install Internet Information Server for the Mailbox Server Role by going to the \Scripts directory on the installation media, and entering the following command:

```
ServerManagerCmd.exe -inputpath Exchange-MBX.xml
```

This will install Internet Information Server and the Failover-Clustering software components according to the Mailbox Server Role prerequisites.

3. Open the graphical setup program (setup.exe) and follow the steps as outlined earlier, making sure that you select the *Custom Exchange Server Installation* and select *only* the **Mailbox Server Role**.

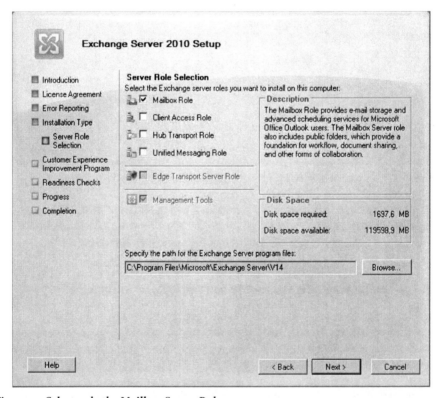

Figure 10: Select only the Mailbox Server Role.

4. During the Readiness Check, a warning message will be displayed about Public Folder Replication as the setup application automatically detects the Exchange Server 2003 environment and the Public Folder existence. Don't worry about this, as Public Folder

replication between Exchange Server 2003 and Exchange Server 2010 will have to be configured manually when setup is finished.

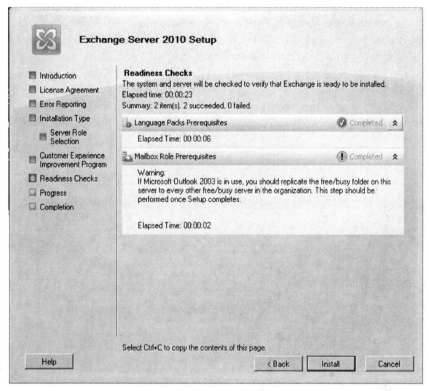

Figure 11: When finished you have to configure Public Folder replication.

5. Click Install to complete the installation process, then click Close on the Welcome screen to end the setup program. As before, you can continue to check the installation using the Exchange Management Console, which is automatically opened after the setup.

3.2.3 Finishing the installation

Now that we have successfully installed two Exchange Server 2010 servers, it's time to configure the environment and finish the setup. We're now going to have to make sure these are taken care of:

•   Public Folder Replication

•   Certificate installation on the Client Access Server

•   Configure Exchange Server 2010 Web Services.

3.2.3.1 Public Folder Replication

During the Mailbox Server Role readiness check, you saw a warning message regarding the Public Folder Replication (see Figure 11). You don't need to worry about this, but you *are* going to have to take steps to ensure that Public Folder information from the Exchange Server 2003 Public Folders is replicated to the Exchange Server 2010 Public Folders, and vice versa.

So, to make sure this happens smoothly, log on to the Exchange Server 2003 server and open the Exchange System Manager. Browse to the Public Folders in the First Administrative Group, and if needed right-click on Public Folders and select "*View System Folders.*" Select the Offline Address Book "*/o=<<yourorg>>/cn=addrlists/cn=oabs/cn=Default Offline Address Book*" and open its properties. Click "*Add*" on the Replication Tab, and add the Public Folder Database on the Exchange Server 2010 Mailbox Server.

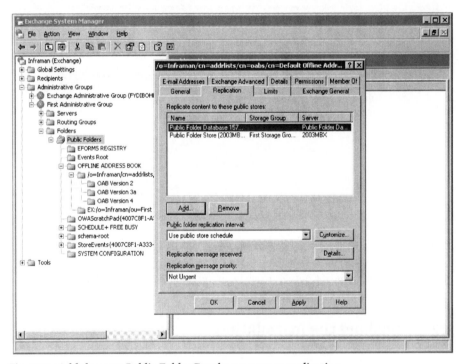

Figure 12: Add the 2010 Public Folder Database to set up replication.

Repeat these steps for:

- OAB Version 2

- OAB Version 3a

- OAB Version 4

- EX:/o=<<yourorg>>/ou=First Administrative Group

- Schedule+ Free Busy: EX:/o=<<yourorg>>/ou=First Administrative Group.

And that's all of your Exchange Server 2003 to Exchange Server 2010 Public Folder Replication set up!

In Exchange Server 2003 you can also use the "Manage Settings" options and perform the above steps at once in a single step.

To setup Public Folder Replication from Exchange Server 2010 back to Exchange Server 2003, log on to the Exchange Server 2010 server and open the Exchange Management Console. In the left pane select *Toolbox*, open *the Public Folder Management Console* in the results pane, and then connect to the Exchange Server 2010 Mailbox Server.

In the Public Folder Management Console, expand the *System Public* folders, and then expand the *Offline Address Book*. For all Offline Address Books located in the results pane, select their properties and configure the replication to include the Exchange Server 2003 Public Folder Database, as demonstrated below:

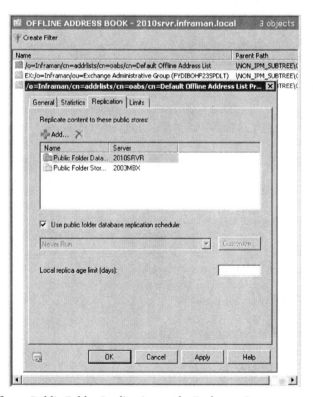

Figure 13: Configure Public Folder Replication to the Exchange Server 2003 server.

All you need to do to finalize your Replication configuration is repeat these steps for:

- OAB Version 2

- OAB Version 3a

- OAB Version 4

- EX:/o=<<yourorg>>/ou=Exchange Administrative Group (FYDIBOHF23SPDLT)

- EX:/o=<<yourorg>>/ou=First Administrative Group

- Schedule+ Free Busy: EX:/o=<<yourorg>>/ou= Exchange Administrative Group (FYDIBOHF23SPDLT)

- Schedule+ Free Busy: EX:/o=<<yourorg>>/ou=First Administrative Group.

Bear in mind that, depending on the size of your Public Folder database, you may have to wait some time for Public Folder Replication to finish.

3.2.3.1 Certificate installation

After installation of the Client Access Server, a new certificate also needs to be installed. By default a self-signed certificate is created during setup but, for production purposes, a third-party certificate is needed. For Exchange Server 2010, a Unified Communication (UC) certificate is used, and these have their own Subject Name (like webmail.inframan.nl) as well as "Subject Alternative Names" like *autodiscover.inframan.nl* and *mail.inframan.nl*. Check out Microsoft knowledge base article 929395 (HTTP://TINYURL.COM/CERTVENDORS) for more information regarding UC certificates, and a list of supported Certification Authorities that can issue them.

Suppose we have a domain called "inframan.nl" – our Outlook Web App name can be *webmail.inframan.nl*. A second namespace used in Exchange Server 2010 is 'autodiscover', which resolves, in our example, to *autodiscover.inframan.nl*. So far this is the same as it was in Exchange Server 2003. New in Exchange Server 2010 is a third name called "legacy" which results in *legacy.inframan.nl*. This legacy namespace is used for interoperability between Outlook Web Access in Exchange Server 2003 and Exchange Server 2010 Outlook Web App. All three names are used on the Client Access Server, so for the Client Access Server, a minimum of three SAN values are needed:

- **Webmail.inframan.nl** (primary OWA access point)

- **Autodiscover.inframan.nl**

- **Legacy.inframan.nl** (OWA access for Exchange Server 2003 mailboxes).

To ensure the Exchange Server 2010 Client Access Server role functions correctly the various settings need to be configured, which is explained in the next section.

3.2.3.3 Configure Exchange Web Services

Like its predecessors, Exchange Server 2010 uses the Client Access Server to offer Offline Address Book downloads and Free/Busy information using the HTTP protocol, and these can be used by Outlook 2007 and Outlook 2010. However, *Outlook 2003* uses the Public Folder architecture to get the Offline Address Book and Free/Busy information.

As explained in Section **3.2.2.2** (See Figure 7. Enter the external domain for your Client Access Server.) you can enter the external domain that the Client Access Server is using, for example *webmail.inframan.nl*. If you haven't configured the external domain during setup, you have to configure the following settings using the Exchange Management Shell command below.

```
Offline Address Book:
    Set-OABVirtualDirectory <2010CASHUB01>\OAB* `
        -ExternalURL https://webmail.inframan.nl/OAB
Web Services:
    Set-WebServicesVirtualDirectory <2010CASHUB01>\EWS* `
        -ExternalURL https://webmail.inframan.nl/ews/exchange.asmx

ActiveSync:
    Set-ActiveSyncVirtualDirectory <2010CASHUB01>\Microsoft-
Server-ActiveSync`
        -ExternalURL https://webmail.inframan.nl/Microsoft-Server-
ActiveSync

Set-OWAVirtualDirectory <2010CASHUB01>\OWA* `
    -ExternalURL https://webmail.inframan.nl/OWA `
    -Exchange2003URL https://legacy.inframan.nl/exchange

Set-ECPVirtualDirectory <2010CASHUB01>\ECP* `
    -ExternalURL https://webmail.inframan.nl/ECP
```

Before the Offline Address Book can be distributed by the Client Access Server, the Generation Server needs be changed from Exchange Server 2003 to Exchange Server 2010. This can be achieved by using the Exchange Management Console as follows:

1. Log on to the Exchange Server 2010 server and open the Exchange Management Console.

2. Expand Microsoft Exchange on-Premises and expand the organization container

3. Click the Mailbox option, and in the results pane select the Offline Address Book tab. The Default Offline Address List will appear, and the Generation Server will be the current Exchange Server 2003 server.

4. Right-click the Default Offline Address Book and select Move. The Move Offline Address Book wizard will appear. Use the Browse button to select the new Exchange Server 2010 Mailbox Server and, when finished, click Move again. When the move to the new Mailbox Server is complete, click Finish.

Note

You can also use the Exchange Management Shell to move the Generation Server to Exchange Server 2010 by using the following command.

```
move-OfflineAddressBook -Identity '\Default Offline Address List'
    -Server '2010SRVR'
```

Even once you've gone through these steps, the distribution itself is still using the Public Folder Mechanism. To change this to Web-based distribution, use the following procedure:

1. Log on to the Exchange Server 2010 server and open the Exchange Management Console.

2. Expand *Microsoft Exchange on-Premises,* and expand the organization container.

3. Click the Mailbox option and select the *Offline Address Book* tab in the results pane. The *Default Offline Address List* will appear. Right-click this and select properties.

4. Select the Distribution tab and tick the *Enable Web-based distribution* check box. Click Add to select the *Client Access Server Virtual Directory* used for distribution and, when finished, click OK.

The Exchange Server 2010 Client Access Server will now start distributing the Offline Address Book using a virtual directory, using the HTTP protocol that can be used by Microsoft Outlook 2007 or Outlook 2010 clients.

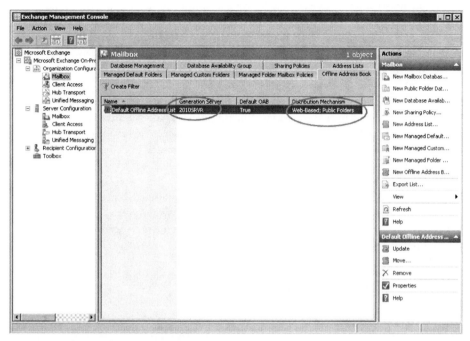

Figure 14: After configuring the Offline Address Book generation server you can check the configuration using the Exchange Management Console.

Users with mailboxes still on Exchange Server 2003, who access their mailbox using a Windows Mobile device, will get an error when they use the Exchange Server 2010 Client Access Server. These users will be able to synchronize their device when the Microsoft-Server-ActiveSync virtual directory on the Exchange Server 2003 back-end server has *Integrated Windows Authentication* enabled. This will allow the Client Access Server and the Exchange Server 2003 back-end server to use Kerberos for authentication.

Now that you've got your Public Folder Replication, Certificates and Web Services all configured, it's time to change your Internet access infrastructure. You need to make sure that users who try to access HTTPS://WEBMAIL.INFRAMAN.NL (the example we've been using so far) are redirected to the new Exchange Server 2010 Client Access Server. So I'll quickly outline the SMTP Infrastructure for this coexistence scenario.

3.2.4 SMTP Infrastructure

As discussed earlier, when an Exchange Server 2010 Hub Transport server is installed into an existing Exchange Server 2003 environment, it installs a special Legacy, or Interop, Routing Group Connector. This Interop Routing Group Connector is responsible for sending messages between Exchange Server 2003 and Exchange Server 2010 and vice versa.

When you move mailboxes to Exchange Server 2010 and a new message arrives on the Exchange Server 2003 front-end server, this server will check Active Directory and find the user's mailbox is on Exchange Server 2010. The message will be routed through the Interop Routing Group Connector to the new Hub Transport Server, and the message will be delivered in the Exchange Server 2010 Mailbox Server – nice and simple.

Similarly, when a user with a mailbox on Exchange Server 2010 composes a message for a mailbox on Exchange Server 2003, the message is routed from the Hub Transport Server, through the Interop Routing Group Connector, to the Exchange Server 2003 front-end server. From there it will be delivered to the user's mailbox on the Exchange Server 2003 Mailbox server – *also* nice and simple.

As this is a completely stable system, it is up to the system administrator to decide when the mail flow is switched from delivery at the Exchange Server 2003 server to the Exchange Server 2010 Hub Transport Server. There are no hard requirements when to switch the message flow.

3.2.4.1 Edge Transport Server

An Exchange Server 2010 Edge Transport Server is used for message hygiene purposes; it will be used as an anti-spam and anti-virus solution. The anti-spam solution is built in to the product, and Microsoft Forefront for Exchange Server can be used for antivirus.

An Exchange Server 2010 Edge Transport Server can also be used together with a pure Exchange Server 2003 environment. The Edge Transport Server is used as a smart host for the Exchange Server 2003 server, and can still act as an anti-spam and antivirus solution. The full feature set of an Edge Transport Server is, of course, not available in an Exchange Server 2003 environment.

The full feature set of the Exchange Server 2010 Edge Transport Server becomes available when you transition to the Exchange Server 2010 Hub Transport Server, subscribe the Edge Transport Server to the Hub Transport Server, and switch the mail flow from the Exchange Server 2003 environment to the Exchange Server 2010 environment.

If you want to install the Exchange Server 2010 Edge Transport Server and subscribe it to the Exchange Server 2010 Hub Transport Server, follow the installation guidelines as outlined in Chapter 2. The question is, do you *want* to install the Edge Transport Server? There's no definitive answer to this, and a consultant's answer would be "it depends." An Edge Transport Server does a great job in offering antivirus and anti-spam functionality and, as such, I can really recommend it. But a lot of customers already have other anti-spam and antivirus solutions that perform very well. If this is the case, you have to make a decision based on experiences, pricing, manageability, etc.

3.2.5 Final Exchange 2003 coexistence notes

So, at the end of that you should have everything you need to configure your own Exchange Server 2003 Coexistence scenario. Just to finish off, there are a couple of things I want to recap for when you are running this kind of scenario:

*   An Exchange Server 2003 and Exchange Server 2010 coexistence scenario has two management interfaces:

    *   The Exchange Server 2003 System Manager can *only* be used to manage Exchange Server 2003 objects.

    *   The Exchange Server 2010 Management Console and Management Shell can *only* be used to manage Exchange Server 2010 objects.

*   If mailboxes running on Exchange Server 2003 need to be moved to Exchange Server 2010, this can *only* be achieved using the Exchange Server 2010 tools.

*   When shared mailboxes are moved from Exchange Server 2003 to Exchange Server 2010, they will continue to run as shared mailboxes. They can be converted to Resource Mailboxes at a later stage.

*   Mailboxes can be moved from Exchange Server 2010 to Exchange Server 2003 using the Exchange Management Console or the Exchange Management Shell on Exchange Server 2010. When a mailbox on Exchange Server 2010 has an archive associated with it, the archive naturally has to be removed before the move to Exchange Server 2003.

3.3 Coexistence with Exchange Server 2007

The differences between Exchange Server 2007 and Exchange Server 2010 aren't that large. All the server roles have new or altered functionality, but it isn't as drastic as the differences with Exchange Server 2003. One of the important changes between Exchange Server 2007 and Exchange Server 2010 are in the replication technology. The "old" replication technology, like Cluster Continuous Replication (CCR), Local Continuous Replication (LCR) and Stand-by Continuous Replication (SCR) are no longer available in Exchange Server 2010. Additionally, in the Client Access Server, the MAPI on the Middle Tier (MOMT) functionality is new when compared to Exchange Server 2007.

When building a coexistence scenario with Exchange Server 2007 the most import issues are:

- **Management Interfaces** – Exchange Server 2010 objects can be managed by the Exchange Management Console (EMC) or the Exchange Management Shell (EMS). Some attributes of an Exchange Server 2007 can be viewed as well, but Exchange Server 2007 objects should be managed using the Exchange Server 2007 Management Tools.

- **Server Role Features** – Exchange Server 2010 has the same Server Roles as Exchange Server 2007, but the functionality that's available to end-users depends or the location of their mailbox. Not all features are available when the user's mailbox is still hosted on Exchange Server 2007.

If you've already read the section about a Coexistence scenario with Exchange Server 2003, then some of the more fine-grained details of this process will seem fairly familiar. Nevertheless, this section of the chapter should give you everything you need to configure a coexistence scenario between Exchange Servers 2007 and 2010. Before I dive into the installation details, I'd just like to make a brief comment regarding 64-bit systems.

3.3.1 64-bit in Exchange Server 2007

Exchange Server 2007 was the first Exchange version available in a 64-bit version, and indeed the 64-bit version is the *only* version that is supported in a production environment. The Information Store of Exchange Server 2007 will use as much memory as is available to cache mailbox information which, in turn, can result in a dramatic reduction of disk I/O. As long as there is sufficient memory available in the Exchange server, of course.

As a result (to be fair, this is somewhat true for ANY server) an Exchange Server 2007 server that is not properly designed will still result in a poorly performing server. A best practice for designing a well performing Exchange server is to use the Exchange Storage Calculator, which is available on the Microsoft Exchange Team Blog: HTTP://TINYURL.COM/STORAGECALC.

There *is* a 32-bit version available of Exchange Server 2007, but this version is *not* supported in a production environment and should only be used in test and development environments. To enforce this, it is time-bombed, and will officially only run for 120 days. But now, on to the installation!

3.4 Installing Exchange Server 2010 into an existing Exchange Server 2007 environment

Before installing the first Exchange Server 2010 server into an existing Exchange Server 2007 environment, a number of prerequisites have to be met:

- All domains in an existing Active Directory forest have to be running in native mode.

- The Active Directory forest has to be running on a Windows Server 2003 forest functionality level.

- Each site in Active Directory should have at least one Domain Controller and the Global Catalog server on a Windows Server 2003 SP2 level. Although not enforced, it is recommended to have 64-bit type Domain Controllers and Global Catalog Servers for optimal performance.

- The Schema Master of the Active Directory needs to be a Windows Server 2003 SP2 or a Windows Server 2008 SP1 server. This can either be a 64-bit or a 32-bit server.

- All Exchange Server 2007 servers must have Service Pack 2 installed.

- The Internet facing Active Directory sites *must* be the first sites that will be upgraded to Exchange Server 2010.

Likewise, the physical server where Exchange Server will be installed needs to meet the following prerequisites:

- The server needs to be a 64-bit (64-bit Itanium is not supported!) based computer.

- Windows Server 2008 SP2 or Windows Server 2008 R2 64-bit needs to be installed.

- Internet Information Server needs to be installed.

- Windows Remote Management (WinRM) 2.0 needs to be installed.

- PowerShell 2.0 needs to be installed.

- .NET Framework 3.51 needs to be installed.

Depending on the version of Windows 2008 you're using (i.e. Service Pack 2 or R2) a number of hotfixes need to be installed. I strongly recommend you bring your server up to date with the latest hotfixes from Windows Update.

3.4.1 Exchange Server 2010 order of installation

Exchange Server 2010 can be installed into an existing Exchange Server 2007 environment in the same forest and the same domain, but there are some issues with compatibility. You have to take the installation order of the Exchange Server 2010 servers into account to minimize the impact of this:

- **First** – *Exchange Server 2010 Client Access Server*. The Client Access Server can work with an Exchange Server 2007 Mailbox Server *as well as* an Exchange Server 2010 Mailbox Server.

- **Second** – *Exchange Server 2010 Hub Transport Server*.

- **Third** – *Exchange Server 2010 Mailbox Server*.

- **The Edge Transport Server can be installed at any time, since an Exchange Server 2010 Edge Transport Server can be subscribed to an Exchange Server 2007 SP2 Hub Transport Server.**

After you've installed the Mailbox Server role and established a proper Public Folder replication between Exchange Server 2007 and Exchange Server 2010, you can start moving mailboxes to the new Mailbox Server. Of course, the Public Folder replication needs only be configured when Public Folders are used in Exchange Server 2007.

Please bear in mind that an in-place upgrade to Exchange Server 2010 *in any scenario* is NOT supported!

3.4.2 Installing Exchange Server 2010

Although there's a specific order to the installation of server roles, these roles can, of course, be combined on one server.

When upgrading to Exchange Server 2010 the following steps need to be performed:

1. Upgrade the Active Directory Schema.

2. Upgrade the Active Directory Configuration.

3. Upgrade the Active Directory Domain.

4. Install the Exchange Server 2010 server roles.

So, let's get started with the upgrade.

3.4.2.1 Upgrading Active Directory

Before you even think about installing server roles, the first step in upgrading the Exchange Server 2007 environment to Exchange Server 2010 is upgrading the Active Directory Schema. Bear in mind that it is also possible to use the graphical setup program, as this can be found on the installation media as *setup.exe*. When you use this program, all steps below are automatically performed. The command prompt system is mainly for people who want to retain more fine-grained control over their transition.

This is not different from the procedure described in Section **3.2.2**, and can also be achieved by entering the following into a command prompt:

```
Setup.com /PrepareSchema
```

Once the Schema has been upgraded, the Configuration (which is stored in the Active Directory Configuration Container) can follow.

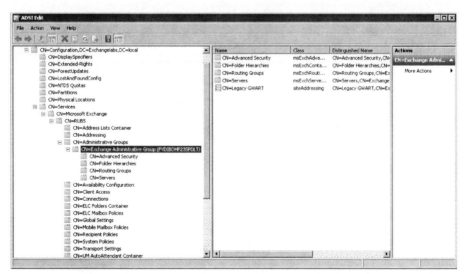

Figure 15: The Exchange Organization in the Configuration Partition of a pure Exchange Server 2007 environment.

The Exchange Server 2007 organization called "RUBS" can be seen in Figure 15. All Exchange Server 2007 servers are stored in the default Administrative Group *Exchange Administrative Group (FYDIBOHF23SPDLT)*. If your Exchange 2007 has previously been upgraded from Exchange Server 2003, then it's very likely that you will see a *First Administrative Group* as well. If the upgrade was finished correctly, this First Administrative Group should be empty, or almost empty.

Exchange Server 2010 *also* uses the *Exchange Administrative Group (FYDIBOHF23SPDLT)*, but there are differences in how Exchange Server 2010 works, for example, with databases. In Exchange Server 2007, a database is bound to a Mailbox Server, while in Exchange Server 2010 databases exists on the organization level, independent of any Mailbox Server. So when upgrading the Exchange Configuration, the Administrative Group is changed to facilitate both the Exchange Server 2007 environment as well as the Exchange Server 2010 environment.

When you want to change the Exchange Configuration, open a Command Prompt, navigate to the Exchange Server 2010 installation media, and enter the following command:

```
Setup.com /PrepareAD
```

After upgrading the Exchange Configuration, some Exchange Server 2010 specific entries appear in the Exchange Administrative Group, like the Database Availability Group and the Databases container. This is more or less what you should see:

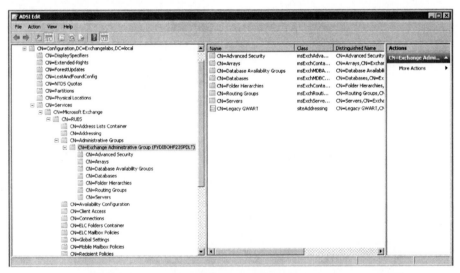

Figure 16: The Configuration Container after upgrading the Active Directory. The Exchange Server 2010 specific entries are clearly visible.

The next step is to prepare the domain (or domains if you have multiple domains that host user accounts with Exchange Server mailboxes) for use with Exchange Server 2010. To do this, open a command prompt, navigate to the installation media and enter the following command:

```
Setup.com /PrepareDomain
```

And if you want to prepare *all* domains in your environment, enter the following command:

```
Setup.com /PrepareAllDomains
```

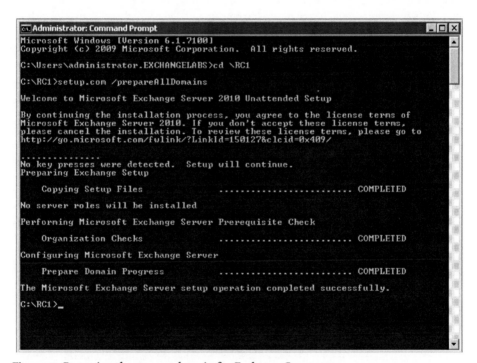

Figure 17: Preparing the current domain for Exchange Server 2010.

When the setup /PrepareDomain is finished, the Active Directory is now ready to install the first Exchange Server 2010 server.

3.4.2.2 Installing the Exchange Server 2010 servers

As mentioned earlier, the *only* supported order of installation of Exchange Server 2010 server roles into an existing Exchange Server 2007 environment is as follows:

- Client Access Servers

- Hub Transport Servers

- Mailbox Servers.

Also, the Internet-facing Active Directory site, the site associated with your external Autodiscover record, should be the *first* to be transitioned. Then you should transition other Internet-facing Active Directory sites. The last sites you should transition are the internal Active Directory sites. Transitioning internal Active Directory sites before the Internet-facing Active Directory sites have been transitioned is *not* supported.

In our test environment, we are installing a combined Exchange Server 2010 Client Access Server role and Hub Transport Server role, and one dedicated Exchange Server 2010 Mailbox Server role.

The procedure to install Exchange Server 2010 in an existing Exchange Server 2007 environment is not very different from when installing into an existing Exchange Server 2003 environment, as described in Section **3.2.2.2**.

First, ensure that Windows Server 2008 Server and all the prerequisite software is installed on the target server. To install Internet Information Server 7 (or 7.5 in the case of Windows Server 2008 R2) and other prerequisites, open a command prompt, navigate to the \Scripts directory in the installation media and enter the following command:

```
ServerManagerCmd.exe -ip Exchange-CAS.XML
```

This will install Internet Information Server, as well as other prerequisites, with the right configuration for the Client Access Server and the Hub Transport Server.

To install the actual Exchange Server roles you can use either the command-line setup or the graphical setup. Right now, we will use the graphical setup program, and to open this setup application you just need to start the *setup.exe* program in the installation media.

1. During the setup, choose the Exchange language option. You can choose to download additional language packs from the Microsoft website, or use the language as available on the DVD. Select "Install all languages from the language bundle" to download additional language information.

2. Follow the setup wizard, and at the *Installation Type* windows select "Custom Exchange Server Installation" in order to select the server roles that need to be installed. Select the Client Access Server Role and the Hub Transport Server Role.

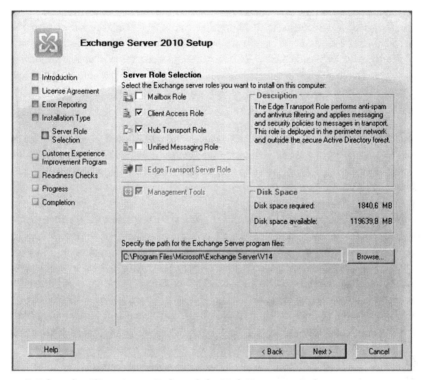

Figure 18: Select the Client Access Role and the Hub Transport Role.

3. In contrast with what I wrote in Section **3.2.2.2**, you are not asked to select a Hub Transport Server in the Exchange Server 2007 environment. This is because both versions use Active Directory sites for routing messages, and so this *should* work right away.

4. Once everything is OK and the Readiness Checks are successful, you can start the actual installation of the Exchange Server 2010 Client Access Server and Hub Transport Server roles. When the setup is finished, close the setup application and reboot the server (if the setup asks you to do so).

5. To install the Exchange Server 2010 Mailbox Server role into the existing Exchange Server 2007 environment you can follow the procedure as outlined in Section **3.2.4**. This is exactly the same, so there's no point in me giving it its own subheading!

3.4.2.3 Certificate installation

After the installation of the Exchange Server 2010 Client Access Server, the coexistence still has to be configured. Eventually, users will connect to the new Client Access Server and, if a user's mailbox exists on the new Exchange Server 2010 Mailbox Server, the request will be processed as usual. When the user's mailbox still exists on the Exchange Server 2007 Mailbox Server, however, the request is either forwarded to the Exchange Server 2007 Client Access Server, or processed by the Exchange Server 2010 Client Access Server, and the information retrieved from the Exchange Server 2007 Mailbox Server. This all depends on the protocol that's being used, but it is important for determining the certificates being used on the Client Access Server as explained below.

Outlook Web Access clients naturally connect to the Exchange Server 2010 Client Access Server. After validating the user's credentials, the Client Access Server checks the mailbox server and, if this is still running on Exchange Server 2007, the request is redirected to the Exchange Server 2007 Client Access Server.

After installing the Exchange Server 2010 Client Access Server, a new third-party certificate needs to be requested. A self-signed certificate is created by default during the setup of the Client Access Server, but this is not at all usable for a production environment. The certificate that ideally needs to be used on a Client Access Server is a certificate with multiple domain names, and these certificates are also known as Unified Communications (UC) certificates. The additional domain names are stored in the "Subject Alternative Names" property of the certificate. For more information regarding these certificates and a list of supported UC certificate vendors, you can visit the Microsoft website: HTTP://TINYURL.COM/CERTVENDORS.

This UC certificate should at least contain the following domain names:

- **Webmail.inframan.nl** – this is the primary entry point for all Outlook Web Access, Exchange Active Sync (EAS) and Exchange Web Services (EWS) requests.

- **Autodiscover.inframan.nl**.

- **Legacy.inframan.nl** – this is the namespace for the Exchange Server 2007 Client Access Server.

If you chose not to enter the external domain during setup (in the case of an Internet-facing Client Access Server) a number of external URLs will also need to be configured as explained in the next section.

3.4.2.4 Configure Exchange Web Services

Exchange Server 2010 uses the Client Access Server to offer the Offline Address Book and Free/Busy information using the HTTP protocol, and these can therefore be used by Outlook 2007 and Outlook 2010. To configure the Exchange services, open an Exchange Management Shell and enter the following commands:

```
Set-OWAVirtualDirectory -Identity 2010CASHUB\OWA* `
    -ExternalURL https://webmail.inframan.nl/OWA

Set-OABVirtualDirectory -Identity 2010CASHUB\OAB* `
    -ExternalURL https://webmail.inframan.nl/OAB

Set-WebServicesVirtualDirectory -Identity 2010CASHUB\EWS* `
    -ExternalURL https://webmail.inframan.nl/ews/exchange.asmx

Set-ActiveSyncVirtualDirectory `
    -Identity 2010CASHUB\Microsoft-Server-ActiveSync `
    -ExternalURL https://webmail.inframan.nl/Microsoft-Server-ActiveSync

Set-ECPVirtualDirectory -Identity 2010CASHUB\ECP* `
    -ExternalURL https://webmail.inframan.nl/ECP
```

In the coexistence scenario, the Offline Address Book generation server is still the Exchange Server 2007 Mailbox Server. We want to move this to the Exchange Server 2010 Mailbox Server, so we follow these steps:

1. Log on to an Exchange Server 2010 server and open the Exchange Management Console.

2. Expand the Microsoft Exchange On-Premises (SERVERNAME).

3. Expand the Organization Configuration container and select the Mailbox option – click the Offline Address Book tab.

4. Right click the "Default Offline Address Book" and select Move.

5. Use the Browse button to select the new Exchange Server 2010 Mailbox Server and click Move.

It is also possible to move the generation server to Exchange Server 2010 using the Exchange Server 2010 Management Shell. On an Exchange Server 2010 server, open the Exchange Management Shell and enter the following command:

```
Move-OfflineAddressBook 'Default Offline Address Book' -Server
2010MBX
```

If your Exchange Server 2007 environment has Public Folders, it is likely that you will want these on your Exchange Server 2010 Mailbox Server as well. The Public Folder database is, in this case, automatically created, but you have to manually configure replication, which is a bit of a hassle.

1.   Log on to an Exchange Server 2007 Mailbox Server and open the Exchange Management Console.

2.   In the Exchange Management Console, double-click the Toolbox. Double-click the Public Folder Management Console in the results pane.

3.   Select the Offline Address Book and, in the results pane, right-click the "/o=<<organization>>/cn=addrlists/cn=oabs/cn=Default Offline Address Book" and then select the Replication tab. Use the *Add* button to add the Exchange Server 2010 Public Folder Database, and then click OK to close the properties window.

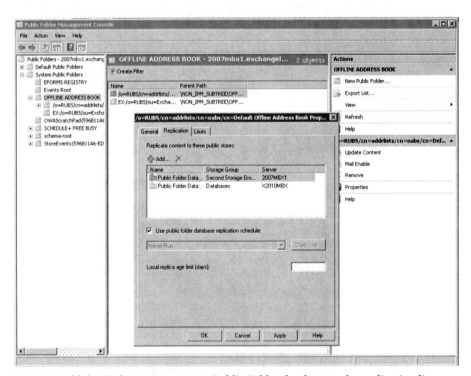

Figure 19: Add the Exchange Server 2010 Public Folder database to the replication list.

Repeat these steps for:

- EX:/o=<<organization>>/ou=Exchange Administrative Group (FYDIBOHF23SPDLT)

- OAB Version 2

- OAB Version 3a

- OAB Version 4

- EX:/o=<<yourorg>>/ou=Exchange Administrative Group (FYDIBOHF23SPDLT)

- Schedule+ Free Busy: EX:/o=<<yourorg>>/ou= Exchange Administrative Group (FYDIBOHF23SPDLT).

3.4.3 SMTP Infrastructure

The Exchange Server 2007 Edge Transport Server needs to be transitioned to Exchange Server 2010 as well. Before doing so, you need to make sure the Active Directory has been transitioned first:

1. Install Exchange Server 2007 SP 2 on all Client Access Servers in the entire Exchange organization.

2. Install the Exchange Server 2010 Hub Transport Server (after you've installed the Exchange Server 2010 Client Access Server!) and subscribe the existing Exchange Server 2007 Edge Transport Server to this new Hub Transport Server. This can coexist for some time if needed.

3. Install the Exchange Server 2010 Edge Transport Server in the DMZ. You can follow the procedure for doing this as outlined in Chapter 2.

4. Remove the subscription from the Exchange Server 2007 Edge Transport Server, and subscribe the new Exchange Server 2010 Edge Transport Server to the Exchange Server 2010 Hub Transport Server.

It's actually rather simple, although you should bear in mind that this is one of the rare cases when the relationship between Exchange Servers 2007 and 2010 is asymmetric! Specifically, an Exchange Server 2010 Edge Transport Server cannot be subscribed to an Exchange Server 2007 Hub Transport Server.

3.4.4 Moving mailboxes to Exchange Server 2010

Mailboxes should be moved from Exchange Server 2007 to Exchange Server 2010 using the 2010 version of the Exchange Management Console, or the Exchange Management Shell. Even more interesting, the new *onlinemove* mailbox functionality (now called *MoveRequest*) can be used, which results in a minimal downtime for the users. Even when they have a multi-Gigabyte mailbox!

During an online move-mailbox, a new mailbox is created on the Exchange Server 2010 Mailbox Server and the contents are synchronized between the old (on Exchange Server 2007) and the new mailboxes. The user is *still working* with the old mailbox and new messages still arrive at the old mailbox. When both mailboxes are in sync the old mailbox is closed, Active Directory is updated with information regarding the new mailbox location and the new mailbox on Exchange Server 2010 is fully up and running.

Lastly, note that the online move-mailbox functionality only works between Exchange Server 2010 servers, and when moving from Exchange Server 2007 to Exchange Server 2010. When moving from Exchange Server 2010 to Exchange Server 2007, the move is offline. It also doesn't work with Exchange Server 2003, which is a shame.

Either way, congratulations! You should now have Exchange Server 2010 running in Coexistence with either your Exchange Server 2003 or 2007 environment!

3.5 Summary

As you've seen in this chapter, Exchange Server 2010 can coexist perfectly in an existing Exchange Server 2003 or Exchange Server 2007 organization. There's no in-place upgrade possibility, so you have to use other (new) hardware to do the actual Exchange Server 2010 installation. When you transition from either version of Exchange Server, be aware that you have to think about the external namespaces, i.e. webmail, Autodiscover and legacy, in advance to get a smooth transition path. In the next chapter I will focus more on the administration part of Exchange Server 2010.

Chapter 4: Managing Exchange Server 2010

Exchange Server 2010 and Active Directory have a closely intertwined relationship; managing an Exchange Server 2010 environment automatically implies managing, to some degree, aspects of an Active Directory environment.

For those not familiar with it, Active Directory can be managed using the default tools, such as:

- the Active Directory users and computers MMC snap-in

- the Active Directory sites and services MMC snap-in

- and the Active Directory domains and trusts MMC snap-in.

Exchange Server 2010 can be managed using:

- Exchange Management Console (EMC)

- Exchange Management Shell (EMS)

- Exchange Control Panel (ECP).

In this chapter, I'm going to focus primarily on getting to grips with the three Exchange Server 2010 management tools, and touch upon the Active Directory methods where relevant.

The Exchange Management Console is the Graphical User Interface (GUI) for managing an Exchange environment. In a Windows environment, especially smaller environments, lots of Exchange Administrators are used to GUIs and, as such, the EMC will almost certainly be the primary means of Exchange Management.

Alternatively, the Exchange Management Shell is also a complete management interface, and can manage all aspects of an Exchange organization. The EMS is actually also the primary management interface, as the EMC is built "on top" of it. Every action taken in the EMC is translated on the fly into an EMS command and executed. Under the hood, the EMS uses Windows PowerShell 2.0 which, combined with the Remote Management capabilities in Windows Server 2008 and Windows Server 2008 R2, gives Exchange administrators the ability to remotely manage their Exchange environment.

As an aside, a combination of the EMC and EMS is a great environment for learning more about using PowerShell 2.0 in Exchange Server 2010, and I'll explain this later when I go into detail about the Management Console.

Exchange Server 2010 also has a new management feature, called the Exchange Control Panel (ECP). The ECP is a part of the Outlook Web App which gives both users and administrators some administrative control. Regular users can, of course, do as much as they were able to in the Outlook Web Access options page in Exchange Server 2007, but Exchange administrators and users with appropriate delegated permissions now have the additional ability to manage some basic information in their Exchange environment.

In this chapter, I'll go through each of these management tools in enough detail for you to pick them up and use them in your own environment as soon as you put the book down. Once I've done that, I'll also take you through some of the finer points of the new Role Based Access Control system, and give you a deeper understanding of Exchange Server 2010's new Archiving and Compliancy features. So without further ado, let's get started.

4.1 The Exchange Management Shell

Windows Server 2008 was the first Operating System that came with PowerShell 1.0 by default, although it was available as a download as far back as Windows Server 2003. In case you don't know about it, PowerShell is a very potent command-line interface which can be used to fully manage your Windows server, and the first Microsoft application to fully utilize it was Exchange Server 2007; the Exchange Management Shell is actually a superset of commands built on top of PowerShell. Product Teams within Microsoft create their own Management Shell solutions, and Exchange Server was one of the first products building theirs. Naturally, there are other tools with Management Shells, such as the System Center products for example, and many of them are also built on top of PowerShell.

Exchange Server 2010 uses PowerShell version 2 (as does Exchange Server 2007 SP2), and in addition to the command-line interface this version also has an "Integrated Scripting Environment," which is an integrated graphical user interface that can be used to easily create PowerShell scripts. As I mentioned earlier, PowerShell 2.0 is also integrated with Windows Remote Management (WinRM), making it possible to use PowerShell to remotely manage your Exchange 2010 environment using the standard HTTPS protocol. All that's needed is a workstation or a server that has PowerShell version 2 installed on the workstation!

Figure 1: The PowerShell Virtual Directory in the Internet Information Snap-in.

Even the Exchange Management Console uses the Management Shell (i.e. is written *on top* of it), and so there are some functions which are not available in the Console but *are* available in the Shell, such as Attachment Filtering in the anti-spam options. As the Exchange Management Shell is the primary management tool in Exchange Server 2010 (as it was in Exchange Server 2007), this development direction may hurt a little bit if you're a diehard GUI administrator.

When the Exchange Management Shell is started, you'll basically see an empty box with just a command prompt – exactly like the Windows command prompt. You can get a list of all available commands at this stage by entering *Get-Command*.

For the benefit of those diehard GUI administrators, a PowerShell command consists of two parts: a Noun and a Verb. Verbs can be instructions like get, set, new, remove, enable, disable etc., and the Noun component can be any objects in Exchange Server. Just combine the Noun and the Verb like this:

- **Get-ExchangeServer** – retrieve a list of all Exchange 2010 Servers in the organization.

- **Set-MailboxDatabase** – set a property on a Mailbox Database.

- **New-Mailbox** – create a new mailbox enabled User.

- **Remove-Mailbox** – deletes a user object and its mailbox.

If you want to learn more about PowerShell commands, a quick web search will turn up scores and scores of learning resources.

Note

Besides the Exchange Management Shell, there's also the Windows 2008 PowerShell on your server or workstation. If you start the PowerShell instead of the Exchange Management Shell, you'll see a Command Prompt with a blue background, and the Exchange Server 2010 cmdlets won't be available. If you are new to PowerShell and the Exchange Management Shell, there will be a day when you start the wrong Shell.

4.1.1 Exchange Management Shell help

If there's anything you're not sure about when you're using the EMS, you have a friend in the form of the Quick Reference Guide, located in C:\Program Files\Microsoft\ExchangeServer\ v14\bin\en\ExQuick.htm. This contains the most important and most-used cmdlets, and their variables.

If you need help on the fly, it's also possible to use the Shell's built-in help function. To get a list of all available help items, just type **help ***. If you need help about a *specific* cmdlet, just type help and the name of the cmdlet. To get help about mail-enabling an existing user, for example, just type **help enable-mailbox**.

4.1.2 Pipelining

Another great feature in PowerShell and the Exchange Management Shell is the *pipelining* function, which uses the output of one cmdlet as the input for a second command. This can drastically reduce the amount of work you need to put in to accomplish relatively complex tasks, and is more or less just limited by your own ingenuity.

For example, if you want to move all mailboxes in a mailbox database called *"Mailbox Database 1988197524"* to another mailbox database called *"Mailbox Database 0823751426"*, you can use the following command:

```
Get-Mailbox -Database "Mailbox Database 1988197524" | New-
MoveRequest -TargetDatabase "Mailbox Database 0823751426"
```

This is what happens:

Get-Mailbox –Database "Mailbox Database 1988197524" retrieves a list of all mailboxes in this particular database. The output of this cmdlet is used as the input of the second cmdlet, the request to online move mailboxes to the other database. It's also possible to use more specific queries. For example, to get a list of all mailboxes whose name starts with "Chris" you would use the following command:

```
Get-Mailbox | where-object {$_.name -like "Chris*"}
```

You can then use this as the input for a request to move all these mailboxes to another database:

```
Get-Mailbox | where-object {$_.name -like "Chris*"} | New-
MoveRequest '
-TargetDatabase "Mailbox Database 0823751426"
```

4.1.3 Bulk user creation in the Exchange Management Shell

This can be very useful, particularly when you need to create a lot of mailboxes in a hurry. Suppose you have an Organizational Unit named "Sales" in Active Directory, where 100 user objects reside. This command will create a mailbox for each user in this Organizational Unit:

```
Get-User -OrganizationalUnit "Sales" | Enable-Mailbox -Database
"Mailbox Database 0823751426"
```

When there are multiple Organizational Units called "Sales" you have to specify the complete path of the Organizational Unit:

```
Get-User -OrganizationalUnit "E14.local/Account/Sales" | Enable-
Mailbox -Database "Mailbox Database 0823751426"
```

It's also possible to filter the output of the Get-User command with the –Filter parameter. For example, to Mailbox-Enable all users whose company attribute is set to "Inframan," enter the following command:

```
Get-User -Filter {(Company -eq "Inframan")} | Enable-Mailbox -
Database "Mailbox Database 0823751426"
```

If you want to be even more specific, for example to Mailbox-Enable all users whose company attribute is set to "Inframan" and whose department attribute is set to "Intern," enter the following command:

```
Get-User -Filter {(Company -eq "Inframan") -AND (Department -
eq "Intern")} | Enable-Mailbox -Database "Mailbox Database
0823751426"
```

The following operations are available for the –Filter option:

- -and

- -or

- -not

- -eq (equals)

- -ne (does not equal)

- -lt (less than)

- -gt (greater than)

- -like (string comparison)

- -notlike (string comparison).

In some cases, you'll find it useful to import a list of users from a .CSV file. This list can be exported from another Active Directory or even from an HR (Human Resources) application. It is actually relatively easy to import a .CSV file using PowerShell; the only thing that you need to be mindful of is that the –Password option doesn't accept clear text input. The input to this field has to be converted to a secure string:

```
$Database="Mailbox Database 1563944384"
$UPN="e2010.local"
$users = import-csv $args[0]
function SecurePassword([string]$password)

{

    $secure = new-object System.Security.SecureString
    $password.ToCharArray() | % { $secure.AppendChar($_) }
    return $secure
}foreach ($i in $users)
  {
  $sp = SecurePassword $i.password
  $upn = $i.FirstName + "@"+ $upn
  $display = $i.FirstName + " "+ $i.LastName
  New-Mailbox -Password $sp -Database $Database
-UserPrincipalName $UPN
  -Name $i.FirstName -FirstName $i.FirstName -LastName
$i.LastName
  -OrganizationalUnit $i.OU

  }
```

On the first three lines, three parameters are set that are used during the actual creation of the user and the mailbox. The file is read in a ForEach loop, and the actual users and the mailboxes are created as this loop progresses.

The *SecurePassword* function reads the password from the output .CSV file and converts it into a secure string which is used, in turn, as the password input during the creation of the users. The .CSV file itself is formatted like this:

```
FirstName,LastName,Password,OU
Jaap,Wesselius,Pass1word,Accounts
Michael,Francis,Pass1word,Accounts
Michael,Smith,Pass1word,Accounts
John,Doe,Pass1word,Accounts
```

To make this script usable, save the script file as "**create.ps1**" in a directory like *c:\scripts*. You'll also need to save the .CSV output file as **users.csv** in the same directory. To actually use the script, open a PowerShell command prompt, navigate to the c:\scripts directory and enter the following command:

```
.\create.ps1 users.csv
```

4.1.4 Remote PowerShell

As I keep saying (I'll stop soon), the Remote PowerShell is new in Exchange Server 2010, making it possible to connect to an Exchange Server 2010 server at a remote location. The workstation doesn't have to be in the same domain or even have the Exchange Management Tools installed – as long as the proper credentials are used, it will work. With this kind of functionality, it's now as easy to manage your Exchange Servers in another part of the building as your Exchange Server in a datacenter in another part of the country.

When the Exchange Management Shell is opened via *Start Menu> All Programs> Exchange Server 2010*, the Exchange Management Shell will automatically connect to the Exchange Server 2010 you're logged on to. But using the remote options, it's also possible to connect to a remote Exchange Server at this stage.

To use the Remote Shell, you'll need to log on to a Windows Server 2008 (R2) server or Windows 7 workstation that has the Windows Management Framework installed. The Management Framework consists of PowerShell 2.0 and Windows Remote Management (WinRM) 2.0, and can be downloaded from the Microsoft website: HTTP://TINYURL.COM/POWERSHELL2.

Make sure that the workstation (or server) supports remote signed scripts. Due to security constraints, this is disabled by default. You can enable this support by opening a Windows PowerShell command prompt and entering:

```
Set-ExecutionPolicy RemoteSigned
```

The next step is to create a session that will connect to the remote Exchange Server. When the session is created it can be imported into PowerShell:

```
$Session = New-PSSession -ConfigurationName Microsoft.Exchange
-ConnectionUri http://E2010MBX01.E2010.local/PowerShell
-Authentication Kerberos
Import-PSSession $Session
```

The PowerShell on the workstation will now connect to the remote Exchange Server using a default SSL connection and, RBAC-permitting, all Exchange cmdlets will be available. It's incredibly easy.

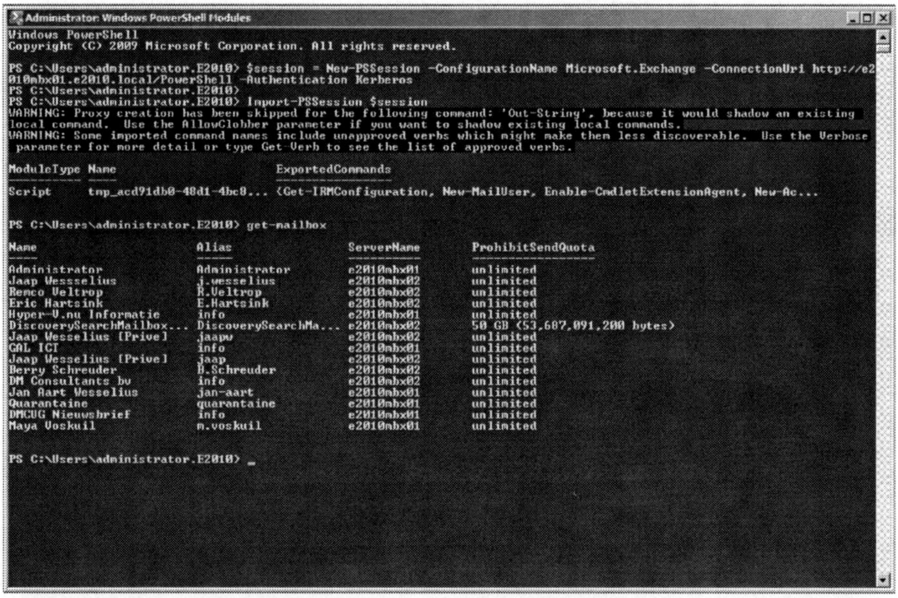

Figure 2: Get Mailbox information on a remote PowerShell session.

To end the remote PowerShell session, just enter the following command:

```
Remove-PSSession $session
```

Admittedly, the above example is from a server that's also a member of the same Active Directory Domain. To connect to a remote Exchange Server 2010 server that's available over the Internet, multiple steps are required. The first step is to create a variable in the PowerShell command prompt that contains the username and password for the remote session:

```
$Credential = Get-Credential
```

A pop-up box will appear, requesting a username and password for the remote Exchange environment. Once you've filled in the credentials, the following command will create a new session that will setup a connection to the Exchange environment. The $Credential variable is used to pass the credentials to the Exchange environment, and then the session is imported into PowerShell:

```
$Session = New-PSSession –ConfigurationName Microsoft.Exchange
-ConnectionUri https://www.exchange14.nl/PowerShell
-Authentication Basic
-Credential $Credential
Import-PSSession $Session
```

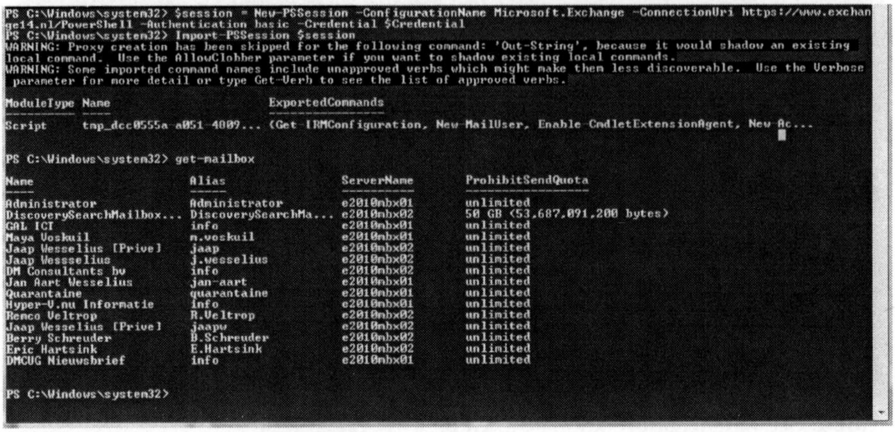

Figure 3: Getting Mailbox information using the Remote PowerShell from an Exchange Server that's somewhere in a datacenter.

Note

If you want to connect to a remote Exchange Server 2010 server over the Internet you have to remember to enable Basic authentication on the remote server. Open the Internet Information Services (IIS) Manager on the server, navigate to the Default Website and select the /PowerShell Virtual Directory. In the results pane, under IIS double-click on Authentication. Here you can enable Basic Authentication.

The examples were for the Active Directory Domain Administrator, who automatically has the remote management option enabled. To enable another user for remote management, enter the following command:

```
Set-User <<username>> -RemotePowerShellEnabled $True
```

4.1.5 Reporting with the Exchange Management Shell

The Exchange Management Shell can actually be very effectively used for creating reports. The EMS has quite a lot of powerful cmdlets, and with the pipelining option it is possible to create all kinds of reporting. I'll give you a few examples, although please bear in mind that the outputs for many of these examples *have* been edited for readability.

The *Get-ExchangeServer* cmdlet will return a list of all Exchange 2010 servers in the organization:

```
[PS] C:\Windows\system32>Get-ExchangeServer

Name          Site          ServerRole   Edition    AdminDisplayVe
----          ----          ----------   -------    --------------
2010CASHUB01  E2010.loc...  ClientAc...  Enterprise Version 14...
E2010MBX02    E2010.loc...  Mailbox      Standard   Version 14....
MAIL          E2010.loc...  Edge         Standard   Version 14....
MAIL2         E2010.loc...  Edge         Standard   Version 14....
E2010MBX01    E2010.loc...  Mailbox      Standard   Version 14....


[PS] C:\Windows\system32>
```

[Edited for readability]

With the –Identity option it is possible to retrieve the information for only one Exchange server, and when the Get-ExchangeServer cmdlet is used in a pipeline with the format-list command, all the detailed information for the server in question is shown:

```
[PS] C:\Windows\system32>Get-ExchangeServer -Identity E2010MBX01
| fl


RunspaceId          : 733756f7-f201-4460-822c-8578f05f8516
Name                : E2010MBX01
DataPath            : C:\Program Files\Microsoft\Exchange
                      Server\V14\Mailbox
Domain              : E2010.local
Edition             : StandardEvaluation
ExchangeLegacyDN    : /o=E2010/ou=Exchange
                          Administrative Group
                          (FYDIBOHF23SPDLT)/
```

```
                              cn=Configuration/cn=Servers/
                              cn=E2010MBX01
ExchangeLegacyServerRole    : 0
Fqdn                        : E2010MBX01.E2010.local
CustomerFeedbackEnabled     : False
InternetWebProxy            :
IsHubTransportServer        : False
IsClientAccessServer        : False
IsExchange2007OrLater       : True
IsEdgeServer                : False
IsMailboxServer             : True
IsE14OrLater                : True
IsProvisionedServer         : False
IsUnifiedMessagingServer    : False
WhenChangedUTC              : 7-9-2009 11:51:56
WhenCreatedUTC              : 27-8-2009 13:14:24
OrganizationId              :
OriginatingServer           : 2010AD01.E2010.local


[PS] C:\Windows\system32>
```

[Edited for readability]

If you want to retrieve mailbox information from your Exchange server, the *Get-Mailbox* and *Get-MailboxStatistics* cmdlets can be used:

```
[PS] C:\Windows\system32>Get-Mailbox

Name              Alias         ServerName    ProhibitSendQuota
----              -----         ----------    -----------------
Administrator     Administ...   e2010mbx01    unlimited
Jaap Wessselius   j.wesselius   e2010mbx02    unlimited
Remco Veltrop     R.Veltrop     e2010mbx02    unlimited
Eric Hartsink     E.Hartsink    e2010mbx02    unlimited
Hyper-V.nu ...    info          e2010mbx01    unlimited
DiscoverySea...   Discover...   e2010mbx02    50 GB (53,68...
Jaap... [Prive]   jaapw         e2010mbx02    unlimited
GAL ICT           info          e2010mbx01    unlimited
Jaap... [Prive]   jaap          e2010mbx02    unlimited
Berry Schreuder   B.Schreuder   e2010mbx02    unlimited
DM Consultan...   info          e2010mbx02    unlimited
Jan Aart Wes...   jan-aart      e2010mbx01    unlimited
Quarantaine       quarantaine   e2010mbx01    unlimited
```

```
DMCUG Nieuwf... info      e2010mbx01    unlimited
Maya Voskuil     m.voskuil e2010mbx01   unlimited
Michael Francis michael    e2010mbx01   unlimited
Katie Pr...(HR) K.Price    e2010mbx01   unlimited
Joe Lawyer      J.Lawyer   e2010mbx01   unlimited
[PS] C:\Windows\system32>
```

[Edited for readability]

To get detailed information about a particular mailbox, the output of that Mailbox's identity can be piped to the Format-List command:

```
[PS] C:\Windows\system32>Get-Mailbox -Identity J.wesselius | fl


RunspaceId                          : 733756f7-f201-4460-822c-
8578f05f8516
Database                            : Mailbox Database
0889073255
DeletedItemFlags                    : DatabaseDefault
UseDatabaseRetentionDefaults        : True
RetainDeletedItemsUntilBackup       : False
DeliverToMailboxAndForward          : True
RetainDeletedItemsFor               : 14.00:00:00
IsMailboxEnabled                    : True
Languages                           : {en-US}
ProhibitSendQuota                   : unlimited
ProhibitSendReceiveQuota            : unlimited
RecoverableItemsQuota               : unlimited
RecoverableItemsWarningQuota        : unlimited
SamAccountName                      : J.Wesselius
UseDatabaseQuotaDefaults            : True
IssueWarningQuota                   : unlimited
RulesQuota                          : 64 KB (65,536 bytes)
UserPrincipalName                   : J.Wesselius@DM-
Consultants.nl
ArchiveName                         : {Online Archive - Jaap
Wesselius}
ArchiveQuota                        : unlimited
ArchiveWarningQuota                 : unlimited
WhenChangedUTC                      : 9-9-2009 15:32:53
WhenCreatedUTC                      : 18-7-2009 18:21:41
OrganizationId                      :
OriginatingServer                   : 2010AD01.E2010.local
```

```
[PS] C:\Windows\system32>
```

[Edited for readability]

The *Get-MailboxStatistics* cmdlet retrieves detailed information about Mailbox usage from an Exchange Server:

```
[PS] C:\Windows\system32>Get-MailboxStatistics -server E2010MBX01

DisplayName        ItemCount   StorageLimitstat   LastLogonTime
-----------        ---------   ----------------   -------------
UCUG Nieuwsbrief   363         BelowLimit         31-8-2009...
Joe Lawyer         0           BelowLimit         9-9-2009...
Hyper-V.nu In...   427         BelowLimit         9-9-2009...
Maya Voskuil       33          BelowLimit         7-9-2009...
GAL ICT            5           BelowLimit
Jan Aart Wess...   14          BelowLimit         6-9-2009...
Quarantaine        164         BelowLimit         9-9-2009...
Administrator      5           BelowLimit         7-9-2009...
SystemMailbox...   1           BelowLimit
Discovery Sea...   4           BelowLimit
Remco Veltrop      6631        BelowLimit         9-9-2009...
Online Archiv...   17813       NoChecking         9-9-2009...
Microsoft Exc...   2           NoChecking
Michael Francis    1           BelowLimit
DM Consultant...   735         BelowLimit         9-9-2009...
Microsoft Exc...   2           NoChecking
Jaap Wesselius     8018        BelowLimit         9-9-2009...
SystemMailbox...   1           BelowLimit
Jaap Wesseliu...   1285        BelowLimit         9-9-2009...
Online Archiv...   368         NoChecking         9-9-2009...
Berry Schreuder    1150        BelowLimit         9-9-2009...
Katie Price (...   6404        BelowLimit         9-9-2009...
Jaap Wesseliu...   26566       BelowLimit         9-9-2009...
Online Archiv...   0           NoChecking         9-9-2009...

[PS] C:\Windows\system32>
```

[Edited for readability]

So the Get-MailboxStatistics cmdlet gives lots of information about usage. To get some real reporting information, PowerShell has an option to convert its output to HTML. So, when you enter the following command...

```
Get-MailboxStatistics -Server 2010MBX01 | ConvertTo-HTML
DisplayName > 2010MBX01.html
```

... nothing is logged to the screen, but an HTML file is created in the directory where the PowerShell is running. Use Internet Explorer to open the output file:

Figure 4: Output of the Get-MailboxStatistics cmdlet redirected to an HTML file.

Using just the DisplayName is not really useful, so let's add some more parameters:

```
Get-MailboxStatistics -Server 2010MBX01 | ConvertTo-HTML DisplayN
ame,ServerName,DatabaseName,ItemCount,
TotalItemSize, LastLoggedOnUserAccount  > MbxInfo.html
```

This will give the following HMTL file:

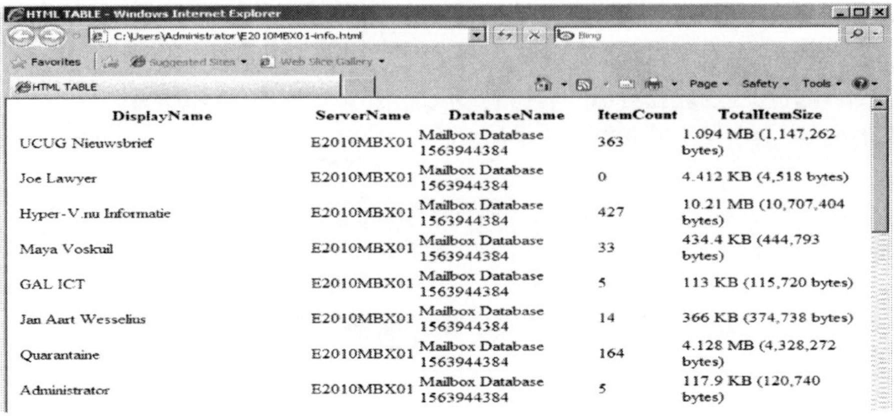

DisplayName	ServerName	DatabaseName	ItemCount	TotalItemSize
UCUG Nieuwsbrief	E2010MBX01	Mailbox Database 1563944384	363	1.094 MB (1,147,262 bytes)
Joe Lawyer	E2010MBX01	Mailbox Database 1563944384	0	4.412 KB (4,518 bytes)
Hyper-V.nu Informatie	E2010MBX01	Mailbox Database 1563944384	427	10.21 MB (10,707,404 bytes)
Maya Voskuil	E2010MBX01	Mailbox Database 1563944384	33	434.4 KB (444,793 bytes)
GAL ICT	E2010MBX01	Mailbox Database 1563944384	5	113 KB (115,720 bytes)
Jan Aart Wesselius	E2010MBX01	Mailbox Database 1563944384	14	366 KB (374,738 bytes)
Quarantaine	E2010MBX01	Mailbox Database 1563944384	164	4.128 MB (4,328,272 bytes)
Administrator	E2010MBX01	Mailbox Database 1563944384	5	117.9 KB (120,740 bytes)

Figure 5: Detailed information about mailbox usage redirected to an HTML file.

Much nicer!

> *Note*
>
> *If you're enjoying pipelining, it's also possible to use the PowerShell Out-File option instead of redirecting using the ">".*

Now let's create a small script with some variables:

- `$Now` contains the date and time the script runs.
- `$BodyStyle` contains a value used to retrieve a stylesheet to customize the HMTL file.
- `$MBXOutput` contains the actual output from the Get-MailboxStatistics cmdlet.

Your script should look something like this:

```
$Now=Get-Date
$BodyStyle="<link rel='stylesheet' type='text/css' href= 'http://
www.domain.com/styles/reporting.css' />"
$BodyStyle=$BodyStyle + "<title>Exchange 2010 Mailbox Reporting</
title>"

$MBXOutput = Get-MailboxStatistics -Server E2010MBX01 |
ConvertTo-HTML DisplayName,ServerName,DatabaseName,ItemCount,T
```

```
otalItemSize,LastLoggedOnUserAccount -Title "Mailbox Overview"
-Head $BodyStyle
$MBXoutput = $MBXoutput -replace "<BODY>", "<BODY><div
id='midden'> <h3>Rapportage $($now)</h3>"
$MBXoutput = $MBXoutput -replace "</BODY>", "</DIV></BODY>"
$MBXoutput | Out-File MailboxInfo.html
```

Save this file as **reporting.ps1** and run the script. It will still show the output of the query, but now it'll be beautifully formatted according the CSS style sheet. This methodology will allow you to create some really cool custom reporting setups.

4.2 The Exchange Management Console

As discussed earlier, the Exchange Management Console is the Graphical User Interface for managing the Exchange Server 2010 environment. The Exchange Management Console is an MMC 3.0 snap-in and consists of several panes (see Figure 6 below).

- **Navigation Pane** – this is the left-hand pane where the Exchange Organization is visible, and it features different leaves like the Organization Configuration, the Server Configuration, the Recipient Configuration and the Toolbox.

- **Results Pane** – this is the middle pane where the results about the selection in the Navigation Pane are visible.

- **Actions Pane** – this is the right-hand pane, where actions that need to be performed against the selections made in the other two panes are chosen.

When the Organization Configuration in the Navigation Pane is selected, the organization-wide configuration of the Exchange Organization can be managed, which all the Exchange servers in the entire organization will share. In the organizational configuration, information can be set for example about Send Connectors, Accepted Domains, Email Address Policies, Database Availability Group, Mailboxes, etc. The Server Configuration in the Navigation pane contains all the server-specific configuration options, such as a particular server's Receive Connectors, Outlook Web App settings or Outlook Anywhere settings.

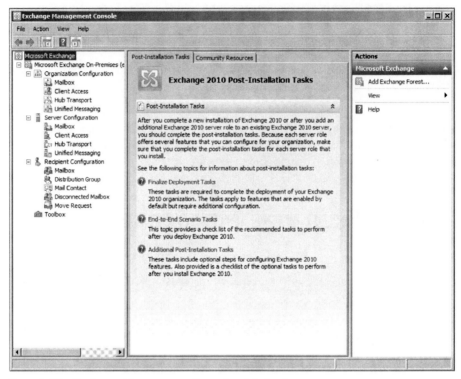

Figure 6: The Exchange Management Console with the three panes.

Lastly, the Recipient Configuration contains all configuration options regarding the following recipients:

- Mailbox
- Distribution Group
- Mail Contact

- Disconnected Mailbox
- Move Request

4.2.1 PowerShell and the EMC

The easiest way to learn the PowerShell commands you'll need to manage Exchange Server 2010 is to remember that, as the Exchange Management Console is written on top of the Exchange Management Shell, every action in the Management Console is translated to a Management Shell command. This is important because it's possible to take an action in the EMC, and then *see its PowerShell equivalent.*

For example, to mail-enable a user in the Management Console:

1. In the Navigation Pane, select the Recipients configuration and select Mailbox. In the Actions pane select New Mailbox.

2. In the New Mailbox Wizard select "User Mailbox," and then click Next.

3. In the User Type Windows, select "Existing user" and click the Add button. Select an available user object (this user object must be already created) and click OK. Click Next to continue.

4. In the Mailbox Settings Windows, enter an appropriate alias for the new mailbox. Click Next to continue.

5. In the New Mailbox window verify the configuration that's entered and click New to create the new mailbox.

All of the configuration information that you've just entered is being translated to a Management Shell command on the fly, and this command is executed then. When the command is executed the window shown in Figure 7 appears.

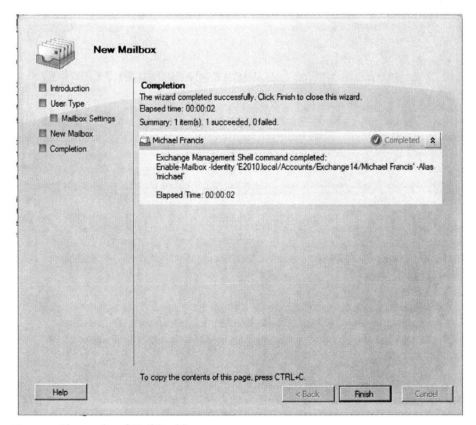

Figure 7: The results of Mail Enabling a user.

In the lower part you see "To copy the contents of this page, press CTRL+C." If you press CTRL+C the contents of this dialog is copied to the Windows clipboard, which contains the following:

```
Summary: 1 item(s). 1 succeeded, 0 failed.
Elapsed time: 00:00:02

Michael Francis
Completed

Exchange Management Shell command completed:
Enable-Mailbox -Identity 'E2010.local/Accounts/Exchange14/Michael
Francis'
    -Alias 'michael'
Elapsed Time: 00:00:02
```

This is the actual command that was executed, and this is by far the easiest way to learn the PowerShell commands.

4.2.2 Evolution of the Exchange Management Console

If you're familiar with Exchange Server 2007, the Exchange Management Console should be familiar as well. There *are* some changes though, primarily because of architectural changes in Exchange Server 2010. Mailbox Databases, for example, are not on the server level as in Exchange Server 2007, but on the organization level. For managing the Mailbox Database, the *Organization Configuration* now needs to be selected instead of the Server Configuration (as is the case in Exchange Server 2007).

Since Mailbox Databases are on the organization level, individual Mailbox Database names must be unique across the entire organization. This is the reason why default Mailbox Databases are created with names like "Mailbox Database 0889073255" and "Mailbox Database 1563944384."

A new feature in the Exchange Management Console is the option to manage multiple Exchange organizations in a single Console (see Figure 9). If you open the Exchange Management Console, by default the Exchange On-Premises organization of which the Exchange Server is a member is shown.

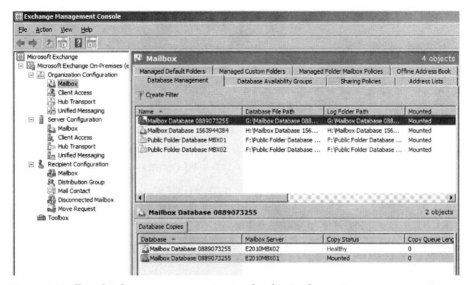

Figure 8: Mailbox databases are on organization level in Exchange Server 2010.

In the Actions Pane, click "Add Exchange forest" and enter the Fully Qualified Domain Name (FQDN) of another Exchange organization you have access to. Enter the proper credentials and two separate Exchange organizations can be managed at once from a single console. The ability to manage multiple locations and multiple organizations is one of the things that Exchange Server 2010 now does very well.

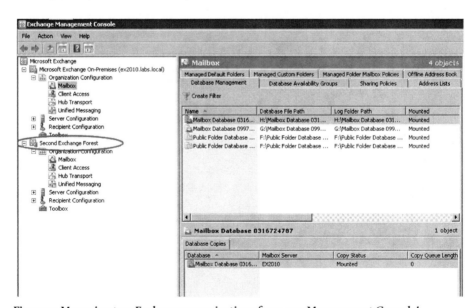

Figure 9: Managing two Exchange organizations from one Management Console!

4.3 The Exchange Control Panel (ECP)

The Exchange Control Panel (ECP) is new in Exchange Server 2010, and is a self-service Control Panel for both end-users *and* Exchange Administrators, accessible through the Outlook Web App interface. The management possibilities available in the ECP naturally depend on the management rights an individual user has in the Exchange organization.

When logged on to the Outlook Web App, click the "Options" button in the upper right corner to access the Exchange Control Panel. A typical user enters a page where only their individual settings can be changed.

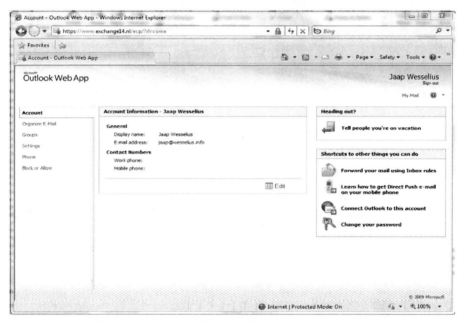

Figure 10: The Exchange Control Panel for a regular user.

Also new in Exchange Server 2010 is the option for the user to change his or her own attributes in Active Directory, such as address, location or phone number. A user just has to click on the Edit button as shown in Figure 10 above, and their personal properties can be changed.

For a typical user the ECP is the replacement of the Options Page in Exchange Server 2007 OWA and earlier, with the additional capability of modifying their personal attributes. However, when a user has administrative privileges, the ECP has much more potential. In the upper left corner there's then an additional option: "Select what to manage," and the available options are:

- Myself

- My organization

- Another user.

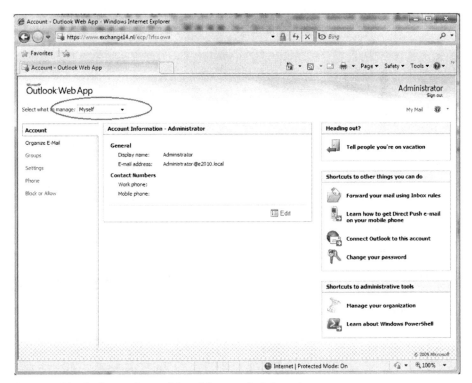

Figure 11: The Exchange Control Panel for an administrative user.

When "My Organization" is selected, the admin user has the ability to perform basic administrative tasks like Managing Mailboxes, Public Groups, External Contacts, Administrative Roles and User Roles. Using the ECP it is even possible to create, modify or delete Mailboxes, Groups or External Contacts.

135

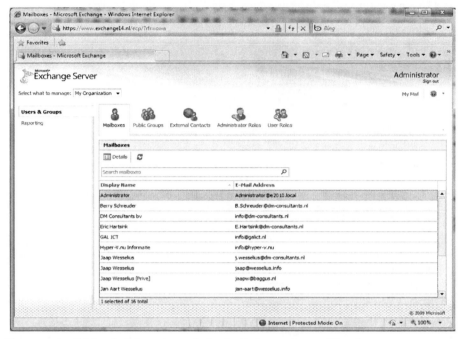

Figure 12: Available administrative tasks in the Exchange Control Panel.

Besides "Users & Groups" there is also a Reporting option available in the Exchange Control Panel, and this gives access to a tool which is the successor of the Message Tracking Tool in Exchange Server 2007. Using the Reporting options it is possible to retrieve information about the message flow in Exchange Server 2010.

To try it out, select the mailbox to search for information, select the Recipient (messages sent to or messages received from) and information for the Subject Line. The Exchange Control Panel will show a list of messages that comply with the search options.

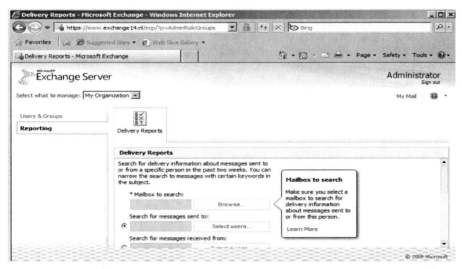

Figure 13: Reporting options in the Exchange Control Panel.

4.4 Role Based Access Control (RBAC)

In Exchange Server 2003 and Exchange Server 2007, the Exchange Administrator has the possibility to perform some "Delegation of Control." This way it is possible to grant other users or security groups more privileges in the Exchange organization, allowing them to perform some administrative tasks as well.

In Exchange Server 2010 this has changed into a Role Based Access model, where users can be added to predefined Role Groups. When a user or a security group is added to such a Role Group they automatically inherit the security rights assigned to it. The following Role Groups are available:

- Delegated Setup
- Discovery Management
- Help Desk
- Hygiene Management
- Organization Management
- Public Folder Management

- Recipient Management
- Records Management
- Server Management
- UM Management
- View-Only Organization Management.

To give a user additional permissions on the Exchange Organization, you really do just need to add the user to the appropriate Role Group. This can be achieved using the:

- Exchange Management Console – the RBAC Editor can be found in the tools section, but when selected you're redirected to the Exchange Control Panel
- Exchange Management Shell
- Exchange Control Panel.

To add a user to the Recipient Management Role group in the Exchange Management Shell, enter the following command:

```
Add-RoleGroupMember "Recipient Management" -Member J.Wesselius
```

To add a user to the Recipient Management Role Group using the Exchange Control Panel, open the ECP and select "*My Organization*" in the "*Select what to manage*" drop-down box. Click the Administrator Roles tab, and double-click the "Recipient Management" Role Group, then click Add and select the user.

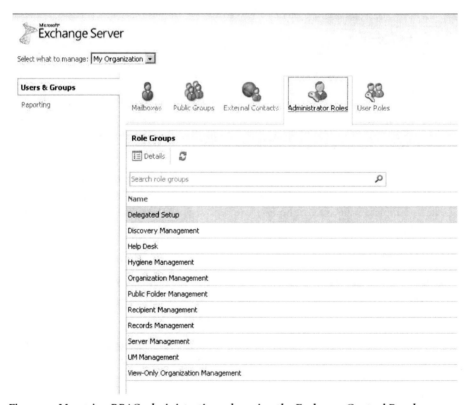

Figure 14: Managing RBAC administrative roles using the Exchange Control Panel.

One of the major benefits of using Role Based Access Control is that it is possible to give very granular permissions to users or security groups. Although this was possible in Exchange Server 2007 as well, you had to work with ACLs to get the same results, and the downside of changing ACLs is that it can give unwanted results due to unexpected restrictions.

4.5 Archiving and compliancy

One important aspect of managing your Exchange environment is obviously managing the email; both the amount of email, and how email is treated.

The amount of email people receive has grown tremendously over the last couple of years. It is not uncommon any more for people to have a multi-gigabyte mailbox, plus a number of PST files where they keep all kinds of information.

Exchange used to be dependent upon an expensive storage solution, although this became less important with Exchange Server 2007. But managing an environment with multi-gigabyte mailboxes brings its own challenges with respect to storage. PST files are a different story again; they're unsafe to use because they are usually stored on a desktop or laptop. If this is stolen, the information is lost and the information is potentially compromised. PST files are sometimes stored on network shares, but this is not actually supported by Microsoft.

Third-party archiving solutions are often implemented, which are a particularly good idea when they're part of an Information Lifecycle Management policy. An Information Lifecycle Management policy is a procedural solution that describes how an organization deals with information (i.e. email). Procedures covered include:

- How organizations adhere to compliancy regulations.

- How long email is stored (retention times).

- Where email is stored (location and folders).

- How email is backed up.

An Information Lifecycle Management solution is a proper business case for an archiving solution. Sometimes "cheap storage" is mentioned but there's no such thing as cheap storage. Of course, a 500GB SATA disk is less expensive than a 146 GB SAS disk, but SATA disks need power, cooling and managing as well. An archiving solution will also need to be managed, backed-up and properly provisioned with hardware (but maybe not as often as a regular Exchange system).

4.5.1 Exchange Server 2010 Archiving

New in Exchange Server 2010 is the built-in archiving solution, making it possible to create a personal archive mailbox within the Exchange organization. To do this, follow these steps:

1. Log on to an Exchange Server and open the Exchange Management Console.

2. Expand the Exchange On-Premise, expand the Recipient Configuration and select Mailbox.

3. In the Results Pane select one or more users that need to have an Archive.

4. Right-click the selected user(s) and select "Enable Archive." Click Yes in the license requirement warning, and the archive will be created.

Except for the icon changing, nothing special happens in the Exchange Management Console. You can request the mailbox properties and select the Mailbox Features tab to check if the Archive is enabled.

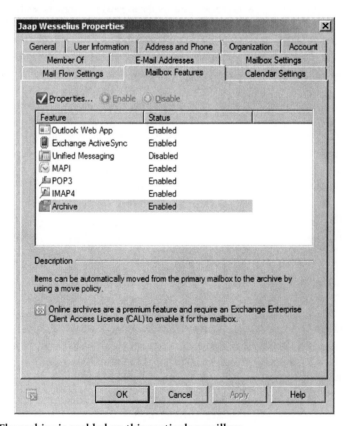

Figure 15: The archive is enabled on this particular mailbox.

The Archive is actually just a secondary mailbox which is created in the same mailbox database as the primary mailbox. To request more information about the Mailbox Archive, open the Exchange Management Shell and enter the following command:

```
Get-Mailbox -Identity <<mailbox>> -Archive | `
    ft ArchiveGuid, ArchiveName, ArchiveQuota
```

The default Mailbox Quota is 2GB, and the default Quota for the Mailbox Archive is unlimited, but these quotas are not set in stone. For example, to set the Mailbox Archive Quota to 10GB, use the Exchange Management Shell and enter the following command:

```
Set-Mailbox -Identity <<mailbox>> -ArchiveQuota 10GB
```

The ArchiveQuota value can be entered using B (Bytes), KB (Kilobytes), MB (Megabytes), GB (Gigabytes) or TB (Terabytes), and the value itself can range from 1 to 9223372036854775807 bytes.

Note

The maximum recommended database size in Exchange Server 2010 is 2TB, so special care needs to be taken with the amount of mailboxes per database and the Archive Quota per Mailbox to prevent unlimited growth of the database.

Creating the Archive Mailbox in the same database as the primary mailbox is always a starting point for a good discussion – is this a good or bad idea? The answer should really be *"neither,"* as Exchange Server 2010 doesn't rely on an expensive storage solution for its databases anymore, and it also supports a JBOD (Just a Bunch Of Disks) solution as well. As long as multiple database copies are configured, Exchange Server 2010 can use 2TB SATA disks for storing a mailbox database and its accompanying log files.

4.5.2 Messaging Records Management

Messaging Records Management (MRM) policies in Exchange Server 2010 are comparable to rules in an Outlook client. With these policies, an Exchange Administrator has the ability to automate the processing of email and simplify message retention. Examples of reasons for implementing MRM rules are things like: your company needs to comply with requirements from Sarbanes-Oxley (SOX), the Health Insurance Portability and Accountability Act (HIPAA), or the US Patriot Act.

With Messaging Records Management it is possible to:

- Configure retention policies on users' mailboxes.

- Configure settings on specified folders so that messages in these folders are sent to another recipient.

One way to implement MRM is by using "Managed Folders," which involves an Exchange Administrator creating one or more custom folders and an associated custom folder policy. This policy can be responsible for, as an example, messages being deleted after 180 or 360 days, but the user is still responsible for moving the individual messages to the custom folder.

Note

Managed Folders and an Archive Mailbox are not compatible. If you are using Managed Folders on a particular mailbox and you want to create an Archive, the creation will fail:

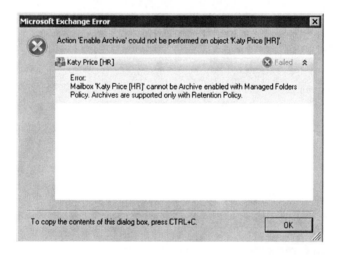

You have to migrate the Managed Folder solution to a Retention Policy solution before implementing an Archive Mailbox.

New in Exchange Server 2010 is the implementation of MRM using "Retention Policies" and "Retention Tags." Retention Tags specify if retention is enabled, how long a message (which can be a note or a contact as well) should be retained, and what action will be performed when the retention age is reached. Messages are processed by the Exchange Mailbox Server based on the retention tags and those tags' content settings. When a message reaches the retention age limit specified in the tag, it can be archived, deleted, or flagged for user attention.

Using Retention Policies, it is now also possible to store only messages with a maximum age of 3 months in the user's mailbox, and store messages older than 3 months in the Archive Mailbox. Suppose there's a Human Resources department within your organization, and all messages older than 3 months should be stored into the user's Archive. The following steps have to be followed:

- Create the necessary Retention Tags which define when an action should be taken (i.e. when the retention time of 3 months have passed).

- Create the Retention Policy that defines what needs to be done when the retention time has passed (i.e. move to the Archive).

- Apply the policy to the mailbox.

Creating the Retention Tags and the Retention Policy cannot be done with the Exchange Management Console, *only* with the Exchange Management Shell. You'll need to open the Management Shell and enter the following command to create the Retention Tag:

```
New-RetentionPolicyTag -Name "move all mail older than 3 months"

   -Type:all      -MessageClass:*
   -AgeLimitForRetention:90
   -RetentionEnabled:$true
   -RetentionAction:MoveToArchive
```

When the tag is created, the results will be shown immediately:

```
[PS] C:\Windows\system32>New-RetentionPolicyTag
-Name "move all mail older than one day" -Type:all
-MessageClass:* -AgeLimitForRetention:1 -RetentionEnabled:$true
-RetentionAction:MoveToArchive


RunspaceId                      : 1a4687cc-cc71-40d1-a487-
edfcf1bc2ff8
IsPrimary                       : False
MessageClassDisplayName         : All Mailbox Content
MessageClass                    : *
Description                     : Managed Content Settings
RetentionEnabled                : True
RetentionAction                 : MoveToArchive
AgeLimitForRetention            : 30.00:00:00
MoveToDestinationFolder         :
```

```
TriggerForRetention                   : WhenDelivered
MessageFormatForJournaling            : UseTnef
JournalingEnabled                     : False
AddressForJournaling                  :
LabelForJournaling                    :
Type                                  : All
SystemTag                             : False
LocalizedRetentionPolicyTagName       : {}
Comment                               :
LocalizedComment                      : {}
MustDisplayCommentEnabled             : False
LegacyManagedFolder                   :
AdminDisplayName                      :
ExchangeVersion                       : 1.0 (0.0.0.0)
Name                                  : move all mail older than
                                        3 months
DistinguishedName                     : CN=move all mail older
                                        than 3 months,
                                        CN=Retention Policy Tag
                                        Container, CN=labs,
                                        CN=Microsoft Exchange,
                                        CN=Services,
                                        CN=Configuration,
                                        DC=labs,DC=local
Identity                              : move all mail older than
                                        3 months
Guid                                  : 3939dc7d-7e3b-4846-9968-
                                        252717fc009f
ObjectCategory                        : labs.local/Configuration/
                                        Schema/ms-Exch-ELC-Folder
ObjectClass                           : {top, msExchELCFolder}
WhenChanged                           : 7-9-2009 12:38:39
WhenCreated                           : 7-9-2009 12:38:39
WhenChangedUTC                        : 7-9-2009 10:38:39
WhenCreatedUTC                        : 7-9-2009 10:38:39
OrganizationId                        :
OriginatingServer                     : 2010AD01.labs.local
IsValid                               : True


[PS] C:\Windows\system32>
```

[Edited for readability]

The next step is to create the actual policy that defines what RetentionTags are included with this policy:

```
New-RetentionPolicy "Move in three months"  `
    -RetentionPolicyTagLinks "move all mail older than 3 months"
```

Again the results will be shown immediately:

```
PS] C:\Windows\system32>New-RetentionPolicy "Move in three
months"
-RetentionPolicyTagLinks "move all mail older than 3 months"


RunspaceId               : 1a4687cc-cc71-40d1-a487-
                           edfcf1bc2ff8
RetentionPolicyTagLinks  : {move all mail older than 3
                           months}
AdminDisplayName         :
ExchangeVersion          : 1.0 (0.0.0.0)
Name                     : Move in three months
DistinguishedName        : CN=Move in three months,
                           CN=Retention Policies Container,
                           CN=labs, CN=Microsoft Exchange,
                           CN=Services,CN=Configuration,
                           DC=labs,DC=local
Identity                 : Move in three months
Guid                     : fe447df8-aba0-48b6-a4da-
                           8061439c7730
ObjectCategory           : labs.local/Configuration/Schema
                           /ms-Exch-Mailbox-Recipient-
                           Template
ObjectClass              : {top, msExchRecipientTemplate,
                           msExchMailboxRecipientTemplate}
WhenChanged              : 7-9-2009 12:40:12
WhenCreated              : 7-9-2009 12:40:12
WhenChangedUTC           : 7-9-2009 10:40:12
WhenCreatedUTC           : 7-9-2009 10:40:12
OrganizationId           :
OriginatingServer        : 2010AD01.labs.local
IsValid                  : True


[PS] C:\Windows\system32>
```

[Edited for readability]

Now the policy with the retention tags needs to be applied to the user's mailbox, in our example, Katy Price from the HR department, and the Managed Folder Assistant needs to be started. To do this, enter the following commands:

```
set-mailbox -Identity k.price -RetentionPolicy:"Move in three
months" -Force
Start-ManagedFolderAssistant
```

When the Managed Folder Assistant has finished applying the policy, you can check the mailbox and its archive. For the user "Katy Price" in our example, the mailbox has shrunk from 1.5 GB to "only" 430 MB. The remaining 1.1 GB of mail data has been moved to the archive.

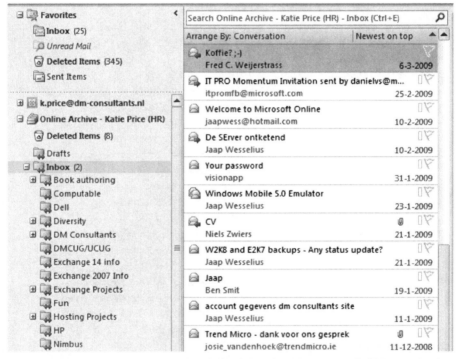

Figure 16: Messages have been moved to the Archive when the Managed Folder Assistant ran the policy.

The Managed Folder Assistant is running on the Mailbox Server where the user's mailbox resides. To change the schedule when the Managed Folder Assistant runs, open the properties of the Mailbox Server in the Exchange Management Console and go to the Messaging Records Management tab. Be careful when you schedule the Folder Assistant to run, especially when a lot of mailboxes are initially managed, and a lot of data needs to be moved.

In that situation, the Managed Folder Assistant will consume quite a lot of resources very quickly.

When creating the Retention Policy Tag using the New-RetentionPolicyTag, the –RetentionAction parameter defines what action needs to be taken when the policy comes into play (In our example, the "MoveToArchive" was selected). The following options are available for the –RetentionAction parameter:

- move to archive

- move to the Deleted Items folder

- delete and allow recovery

- permanently delete

- mark as past retention limit.

Whether the tag applies to the entire mailbox or a specified default folder is determined by the tag's Type property. You can create default policy tags of the following types:

- All
- Calendar
- Contacts
- DeletedItems
- Drafts
- Inbox
- JunkMail
- Journal

- Notes
- Outbox
- SentItems
- Tasks
- RssSubscriptions
- SyncIssues
- ConversationHistory

4.5.3 Discovery

Exchange Server 2010 Discovery is the process of searching relevant content in Exchange Server Mailboxes. Reasons for using the Exchange Server 2010 Discovery can be:

- Legal Discovery

- Internal Investigations

- Human Resources.

Exchange Server 2010 Discovery leverages the content indexes that are created as part of the Exchange Search engine. No doubt, as you use Exchange Server 2010, you'll find plenty more reasons to use this powerful search technology.

To create and manage a discovery search, a user needs to be a member of the Discovery Management Role Group, which is one of the RBAC roles. This is an explicit right, and Exchange administrators do not have sufficient rights to create and manage discovery searches.

Note

Exchange Server 2010 Discovery is a very powerful feature. Users who are members of the Discovery Management Role Group can search through all content in all mailboxes throughout the entire Exchange organization.

To add a user named "Joe Lawyer" to the Discovery Management Role Group, open an Exchange Management Shell command window and enter the following command:

```
Add-RoleGroupMember "Discovery Management" -User "Joe Lawyer"
```

Now this user can create queries to find relevant information if there are suspicions against another employee. To create a discovery search in the Exchange Management Shell enter the following command:

```
New-MailboxSearch -Name "Exchange14 security case 1" -StartDate
"1/1/2009"
-EndDate "08/31/2009" -TargetMailbox "J.Lawyer"
-SearchQuery "Exchange14" -MessageTypes Email -SourceMailbox
"J.Wesselius"


-IncludeUnsearchableItems
```

Note

*The **New-MailboxSearch** cmdlet is only available on the Exchange Server 2010 Mailbox Server role.*

If the –SourceMailbox option is omitted, all Mailbox Databases in the entire Exchange organization will be searched. This can create an enormous result set, producing an unexpected growth of the target mailbox.

```
[PS] C:\Windows\system32>New-MailboxSearch -Name "Exchange14
security case 1"
-StartDate "1/1/2009" -EndDate "08/31/2009"
-TargetMailbox "Discovery Search Mailbox" -SearchQuery
"Exchange14"
-MessageTypes Email -SourceMailbox J.Wesselius
-IncludeUnsearchableItems


RunspaceId                     : 93be590f-a8b8-48f3-944c-
                                 b0f979d4f7f5
Identity                       : f3bdf597-81a1-4ece-b050-
                                 344229f5f57f
Name                           : Exchange14 security case 1
CreatedBy                      : E2010.local/Users/Administrator
SourceMailboxes                : {E2010.local/Accounts/DM-
                                 Consultants-nl/Jaap Wessselius}
TargetMailbox                  : E2010.local/Users/
                                 DiscoverySearchMailbox
                                 {D919BA05-46A6-415f-80AD-
                                 7E09334BB852}
SearchQuery                    : Exchange14
Language                       : nl-NL
Senders                        : {}
Recipients                     : {}
StartDate                      : 1-1-2009 1:00:00
EndDate                        : 31-8-2009 2:00:59
MessageTypes                   : {email}
SearchDumpster                 : True
IncludeUnsearchableItems       : True
DoNotIncludeArchive            : False
LogLevel                       : Basic
StatusMailRecipients           : {}
Status                         : InProgress
LastRunBy                      : E2010.local/Users/Administrator
LastStartTime                  : 10-9-2009 9:11:00
NumberMailboxesToSearch        : 0
PercentComplete                : 0
ResultNumber                   : 0
ResultSize                     : 0 B (0 bytes)
```

```
ResultSizeEstimate        : 0 B (0 bytes)
ResultSizeCopied          : 0 B (0 bytes)
ResultsLink               :
Errors                    : {}


[PS] C:\Windows\system32>
```

[Edited for readability]

The progress of the Discovery Search can be monitored using the *Get-MailboxSearch* cmdlet.

When the search is complete you can log on to the target mailbox, in this example, J.Lawyer's mailbox. The results will be shown in a new folder in the Mailbox:

Figure 17: The results of a Mailbox Search.

When the Mailbox Search is removed using the *Remove-MailboxSearch* cmdlet the folders in the target mailbox will be deleted as well. It's worth bearing in mind, if you're not comfortable using PowerShell, that the ECP can also be used to generate a search.

4.5.4 Litigation hold

In Exchange Server 2010 it is possible to configure a mailbox in "litigation hold." By placing a mailbox in litigation hold you can monitor the mailbox for deleted items, and all changes (i.e. deletions) will be recorded. Deleted and changed items will be returned in a Discovery Search. Litigation hold works for both the Active Mailbox as well as the Mailbox Archive.

To place a mailbox in litigation hold, enter the following Exchange Management Shell command:

```
Set-Mailbox J.Wesselius -LitigationHoldEnabled $true
```

4.6 Summary

There are multiple ways to manage your Exchange Server 2010 environment, and you'll have to see for yourself which is the most comfortable for your own situation. The Exchange Management Console is the most convenient, but for the nitty gritty details you really do have to use the Exchange Management Shell. The new Exchange Control Panel also gives administrators the option of a web interface for basic management interfaces, so you really are spoilt for choice.

This chapter should give you everything you need to start managing your Exchange Server 2010 environment as effectively and smoothly as possible. I've covered the steps you'll need to take to use the more prominent features, and hopefully given you enough tips and helpful notes that you'll have a really good understanding of what's happening to your system. I'd love to be able to dive into really deep detail on all the management and messaging features in Exchange Server 2010, like the improved Messaging Records Management, but if I did that this book would be a real door-stop! I'll just say that everything I've touched upon, such as the personal archive and the retention options, gives you unprecedented possibilities for managing your messaging environment.

Chapter 5: High Availability in Exchange Server 2010

5.1 The background

There are several layers in Exchange Server 2010 that can be configured as a high availability solution. New in Exchange Server 2010 is the Database Availability Group offering high availability on the Mailbox Server role. If you want a full high availability solution, the Client Access Server and the Hub Transport Server need to be configured as a high availability solution as well. This chapter focuses a lot on configuring the Mailbox Server role, as this contains a lot of new features and technologies. There's not too much focus on configuring the Client Access Server role and the Hub Transport Server role as this hasn't changed significantly since Exchange Server 2007.

Before I start with the Database Availability Group, I want to give a database technology primer, just to make the Database Availability Group more understandable.

It is also worth bearing in mind that Exchange Server 2010 Standard Edition now also supports replication technologies, just like the Exchange Server 2010 Enterprise Edition. The only difference is that the Standard Edition only supports up to 5 databases per server, while the Enterprise Edition supports up to *100 databases* per server. This is a perfect development for organizations that do not have thousands of mailboxes, and which therefore do not need to create a lot of Mailbox Databases.

5.2 Exchange Server database technologies

You may feel that my coverage of non-mailbox High Availability is going to be pretty brief. This is because configuring High Availability for these other server roles has not significantly changed since exchange 2007, so I will just give an overview of these requirements. However, before we start talking about High Availability on the Mailbox Server role we have to discuss some database technologies used in Exchange Server 2010. Exchange Server 2010 uses a database to store the primary data, i.e. the messages you send and receive. This database technology is a transactional system, which is pretty common, but Exchange Server uses its own technology built on the Extensible Storage Engine (ESE), sometimes referred to as a JET database.

When installing an Exchange Server 2010 Mailbox Server, the initial mailbox database is, by default, stored on the local C:\ drive; more specifically on *C:\Program Files\Microsoft\ Exchange Server\V14\Mailbox\Mailbox Database <<random number>>*. This random number is generated by Exchange Server during the initial configuration because the database names on Exchange 2010 and higher servers must be unique within the Exchange organization.

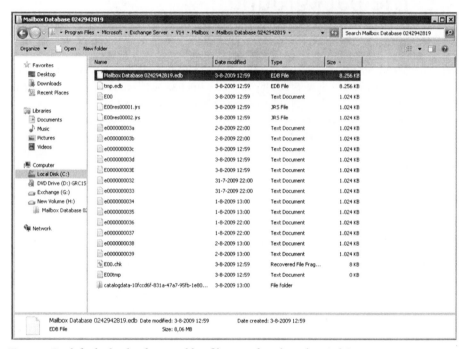

Figure 1: By default the database and log files are placed on the c:\ drive.

A number of files make up the Exchange 2007 database environment:

- "mailbox database 0242942819.edb"

- E00.log

- E000000003a.log, E000000003b.log, E000000003c.log, etc.

- E00.chk

- E00res00001.log and E00res00002.log

- E00tmp.log

- Tmp.edb.

Note

The random number in this example is 0242942819, hence the name of the Mailbox Database is "mailbox database 0242942819.edb."

All names in the above mentioned list start with the same three digits: E00; this is called the database prefix. The first database in the Exchange organization has a prefix of E00, the second database has a prefix E01, and so on.

All of these files play a crucial role in the correct functioning of Exchange server.

A crucial step in understanding Exchange database technology is understanding the flow of data between the Exchange Server and the database itself. Data is processed in 32 KB blocks, also called "pages." When Exchange is finished processing such a page it is immediately written to a log file if it was updated. The page is still kept in memory until Exchange needs this memory again, but when the page isn't used for some time, or when Exchange needs to force an update during a checkpoint, the page is written to the database file. So, the data in the log files is always in advance of the data in the database. This is an important step to remember when troubleshooting database issues!

Note

Exchange Server 2010 uses 32KB pages, Exchange Server 2007 uses 8KB pages, Exchange Server 2003 and earlier use 4KB pages when processing data. The parts of the server memory that are used by these pages are referred to as the "cache buffers."

As data is written to the database, a pointer called the *checkpoint* is updated to reflect the new or updated page that was written to the database. The checkpoint is stored in a special file called the *checkpoint file*, which Exchange Server uses to make sure it knows what data has been written to the database, and what data is in the log files and not yet written to the database. So, in short:

1. Mail data is initially processed in memory, separated into pages.

2. Updated pages are written to the log file.

3. If pages are no longer needed by Exchange these pages are written to the database.

4. The checkpoint file is updated to reflect the new location of the checkpoint.

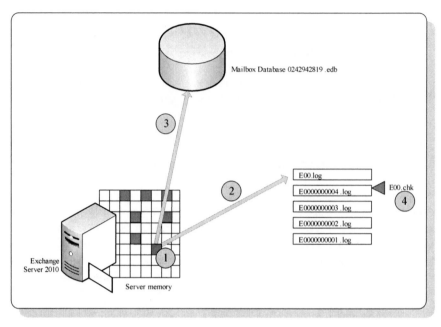

Figure 2: Processing of mail data in Exchange Server 2010.

5.2.1 Extensible Storage Engine

The database engine used by Exchange Server is a quite special, and is built on the Extensible Storage Engine, or ESE. ESE exists in several flavors:

- ESE97 for Exchange Server 5.5

- ESE98 for Exchange Server 2000/2003

- ESENT for Active Directory

- ESE for Exchange Server 2007 and Exchange Server 2010.

ESE is a low-level database engine. This means it knows all about "base types," such as short, string, long, longlong, systime, etc., but it has no knowledge of any structure or schema. The schema is defined by the Information Store in the application. This is in contrast to a relational database like Microsoft SQL server, where all the database structures are just meta-data (i.e. are part of the database itself).

ESE is optimized for handling large amounts of semi-structured data, as it is impossible for an Exchange Server to predict what kind of data will be received, how large the data will be, or what attachments messages will have.

Note

Ever since the early days of Exchange, rumors have been going around about the use of Microsoft SQL server as the database engine for Exchange Server. Microsoft tried this for Exchange Server 2010 and actually got it working. However, the decision was made to stay on the ESE database. More information about this can be found on the Microsoft Exchange Product Group blog: HTTP://TINYURL.COM/ESEDB.

5.2.2 Log files

When Exchange server is working with a page, and that page's status is changed from dirty to clean, the page is written to the log file almost immediately. Data held in memory is fast to access, but volatile; all it takes is a minor hiccup in the server, and data in memory is lost. When it is saved in the log file, the whole server could burn down, and as long as you keep the disk, you also keep the data. Thankfully, saving to the log file is normally a matter of milliseconds. The log files are numbered internally, and this number (referred to as the lGeneration number) is used for identifying the log files, and for storing them on the disk when they are completely filled with data. w

The current log file, or the "log file in use" is E00.log, and while Exchange is filling this log file with data, a temporary E00tmp.log file is already created (or is in the process of being created) in the background. When the E00.log is eventually filled with data, it is saved under another name. The name is derived from the log file's prefix (E00, E01, E02, etc.) and the lGeneration number, which is a sequential hexadecimal notation. So, for example, when the lGeneration number is 1, the E00.log is saved as E000000001.log. Alternatively, the last time this process happened in Figure 1, the lGeneration number was 3E, so the log file was saved as E000000003E.log. Since the lGeneration number is a sequential number, we know that the *next* lGeneration number of the E00.log must be 3F, and the next time this *log file roll-over* process takes place, the log file will be saved as E000000003F.log.

Although it's not directly visible, the lGeneration number is stored inside the log file, and can be checked by dumping the header information of the log file with the ESEUTIL utility. The first few lines of the log file's header should read something like:

```
Base name: E00
Log file: E00.log
lGeneration: 63 (0x3F)
Checkpoint: (0x3F,8,16)
```

The lGeneration number is listed on the third line, both in decimal and hexadecimal notation. Unfortunately, this is very confusing, and there *will* be a day that an Exchange administrator mixes up these notations and starts working with the wrong log file.

After the pages are written to the log file, they are kept in memory, thereby saving an expensive read from disk action when Exchange Server needs the page again. When the Mailbox Server needs that memory for other pages, or when the page stays in memory for a long time, it is written to the database file. This is also known as the "lazy writer mechanism." A common misbelief is that data is read from the log files and written to the database file, but this is not the case. It is written directly from memory to the database, and log files are only read in recovery scenarios, for example, after an improper shutdown of the server. Under normal circumstances, the log files are 100% write, whereas the database is a random mix between read and write actions.

To be honest, it would be possible to write an entire book just about the storage technologies involved, but I think that level of detail generally isn't necessary for the average SysAdmin. However, if you're feeling particularly advanced, I can recommend the book "*Mission-Critical Microsoft Exchange 2003: Designing and Building Reliable Exchange Servers*" by Jerry Cochran. You can find it on Amazon, and Jerry has an article on **WindowsITPro.com** which also covers the topic: HTTP://TINYURL.COM/JERRYCOCHRAN.

5.2.3 Checkpoint files

The relationship between writing data in the log files and writing data into the database itself is managed by the checkpoint file, E00.chk. The checkpoint file points to the page in the database that was last written, and is advanced as soon as Exchange writes another page from memory to the database.

The difference between the data in the database and the data in the log files is referred to as *checkpoint depth*. This checkpoint depth can be several log files; in fact, the default checkpoint depth is 20 log files. By using the checkpoint, Exchange waits before writing to the database, and tries to combine several write actions so that the database write operations can be performed more efficiently.

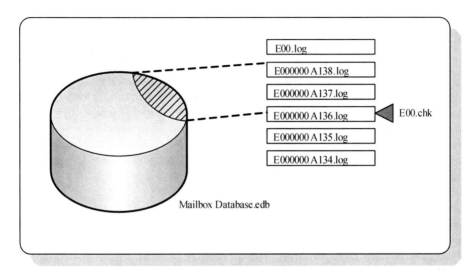

Figure 3: All data below the checkpoint is written to the database.

Checkpoint depth is also a per database setting. So when a database's checkpoint depth is 20 log files, a minimum of 20 MB of data is kept in memory for that specific database. When using 30 databases in Exchange Server 2010, each at its maximum checkpoint depth, approximately 600 MB of Exchange data is kept in memory.

5.2.4 The Mailbox Database

The "*mailbox database 0242942819.edb*" file is the primary repository of the Exchange Server 2010 Mailbox Server role. In Exchange Server 2007 this file was called "*mailbox database. edb,*" whereas in Exchange 2003 and Exchange 2000 the database was comprised of two files: *priv1.edb* and *priv1.stm*. In Exchange Server 2010, a Mailbox Server can now hold up to 100 databases.

The maximum size of an ESE database can be huge. The upper limit of a file on NTFS is 64 Exabytes, and this is generally considered sufficient to host large Mailbox Database files. The Microsoft-recommended maximum file-size of the Mailbox Database on Exchange Server 2010 is 2TB. Compared to the 200GB file-size limit in Exchange 2007 (using Continuous Cluster Replication) this is a tremendous increase. Bear in mind that a prerequisite for using this sizing is that you have to configure multiple database copies to achieve a High Availability solution.

5.3 Developments in High Availability

Ever since Exchange Server 5.5, Microsoft has offered the option to use Windows Clustering to create a highly available Exchange Mailbox environment. In a typical shared-storage cluster environment there are two server nodes available, both running Exchange Server, and both servers are connected to a shared storage solution. In the early days, this shared storage was built on a shared SCSI bus and later on, SANs with a Fiber Channel or iSCSI network connection were used. The important part was the shared storage where the Exchange Server databases were located.

At any given point in time only one server node is the *"owner"* of this shared data, and it is this server node that is providing the client services; this server node is also known as the *active node*. The other node was not able to access this data, and was therefore the *passive node*. A private network between the two server nodes is used for intra-cluster communications, such as a heartbeat signal, allowing both nodes to determine the state of the cluster, and if other nodes are still alive.

In addition to the two nodes, an *"Exchange Virtual Server"* was created as a cluster resource (note that this has nothing to do with virtual machines!). This is the resource that (Outlook) clients connect to in order to get access to their mailboxes. When the active node fails, the passive node takes over the Exchange Virtual Server, which then continues to run. Although users will notice a short downtime during the fail-over, it is an otherwise seamless experience, and no action is needed from an end-user perspective.

Although this solution offers redundancy, there's still a single point of failure: the shared database of the Exchange server. In a typical environment this database is stored on a SAN, and by its nature a SAN is a highly available environment. But when something *does* happen to the database, a logical failure for example, the database is unavailable for *both* nodes, resulting in total unavailability.

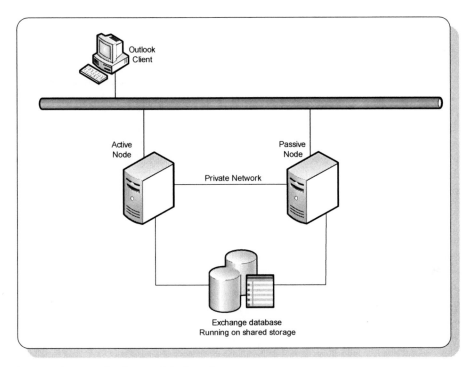

Figure 4: A two node cluster with shared storage.

5.3.1 Exchange database replication

Microsoft offered a new solution in Exchange Server 2007 to create highly available Exchange environments: database replication. When using database replication, a copy of a database was created, resulting in database redundancy. This technology was available in three flavors:

- **Local Continuous Replication (LCR)** – a copy of the database is created on the same server.

- **Cluster Continuous Replication (CCR)** – a copy of the database is created on another node in a Windows failover cluster (there can only *be* two nodes in a CCR cluster).

- **Stand-by Continuous Replication (SCR)** – this came with Exchange Server 2007 SP1. A copy of a database is created on any other Exchange server (i.e. not necessarily in the cluster). This is not meant as a high availability solution, but more as a disaster recovery solution.

This is how database replication works in a CCR clustered environment:

Exchange Server 2007 is installed on a Windows Server 2003 or Windows Server 2008 Fail-over cluster. There's no shared storage in use within the cluster, but each node has its own storage. This can be either on a SAN (fibre channel or iSCSI) or Direct Attached Storage (DAS) – i.e. local physical disks.

As mentioned earlier, the active node in the cluster is servicing client requests, and Exchange Server uses the standard database technology with a database, log files, and a checkpoint file. When Exchange Server is finished with a log file, the log file is sent immediately to the passive node of the cluster. This can either be via a normal network connection or via a dedicated replication network.

The passive node receives the log file and checks it for errors. If none are found, the data in the log file is relayed into the passive copy of the database. This is an asynchronous process, meaning the passive copy is always a couple of log files behind the active copy, and so information is "missing" in the passive copy.

In this environment, *all* messages are sent via a Hub Transport Server, even internal messages. The Hub Transport Server keeps track of these messages in a CCR environment, and can therefore send missing information (which the passive node actually requests) to the passive copy of the cluster in case of a cluster fail-over. This is called the *"Transport Dumpster"* in a Hub Transport Server.

This kind of replication works very well; a lot of System Administrators are using CCR replication and are very satisfied with it. There are a couple of drawbacks, though:

• An Exchange Server 2007 CCR environment is running on Windows Server 2003 or Windows Server 2008 clustering. For many Exchange administrators this brings a lot of additional complexity to the environment.

• Windows Server 2003 clustering in a multi-subnet environment is nearly impossible, although this has improved (but is still not perfect) in Windows Server 2008 failover-clustering.

• Site Resilience is not seamless.

• CCR clustering is only possible in a two node environment.

• All three kinds of replication (LCR, CCR and SCR) are managed differently.

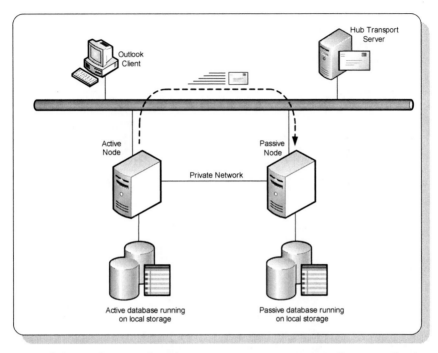

Figure 5: A fail-over cluster with Exchange Server 2007 Continuous Cluster Replication.

To overcome these issues, Microsoft has dramatically improved the replication technology, and reduced the administrative overhead at the same time. This is achieved by completely hiding the cluster components behind the implementation of Exchange Server 2010. The cluster components are still there, but the administration is completely done with the Exchange Management Console or the Exchange Management Shell.

5.3.2 Database Availability Group and Continuous Replication

In Exchange Server 2010, Microsoft introduces the concept of a Database Availability Group or DAG, which is a logical unit of Exchange Server 2010 Mailbox Servers. All Mailbox Servers within a DAG can replicate databases to each other, and a single DAG can hold up to 16 Mailbox Servers and up to 16 copies of a database. The idea of multiple copies of a database in one Exchange organization is called *Exchange Mobility*; one database exists on multiple servers, each instance of which is 100% identical and thus has the same GUID.

With a DAG in place, clients connect to an Active Database, which is the database where all data is initially stored. Also, new SMTP messages that arrive, either from outside or inside the organization, are stored in this database first. When the Exchange Server has finished processing information in the database's log file, the file is replicated to other servers (you can assign which servers should have a copy of the database). The log file is inspected upon receipt and, if everything is all right, the information contained in the log file is dropped into the local copy of the database.

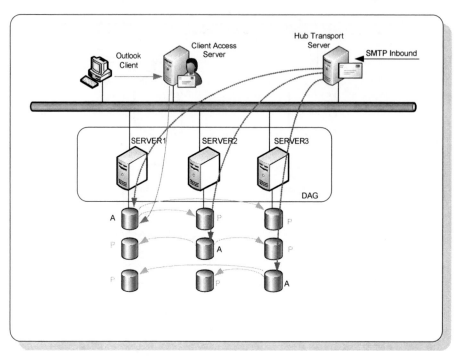

Figure 6: A Database Availability Group with three servers; each server holds one Active Database and two Passive Databases.

In Exchange Server 2010, all clients connect to the Client Access Server, including all MAPI clients like Microsoft Outlook. Supported Outlook clients in Exchange Server 2010 include Outlook 2003, Outlook 2007 and Outlook 2010. So, the Outlook client connects to the Client Access Server which, in turn, connects to the mailbox in the Active Copy of the database, as you can see in Figure 6. Unfortunately, this is only true for Mailbox Databases. When an Outlook client needs to access a Public Folder Database, the client still accesses the Mailbox Server directly.

When the active copy of a database or its server fails, one of the passive copies of the database becomes active. The order of fail-over is configurable during the configuration of database copies. The Client Access Server automatically notices the fail-over, and starts using the new Active Database. Since the Outlook client is connected to the Client Access Server and not directly to the database, a database fail-over is fully transparent. Messages like "The connection to the server was lost" and "The connection to the server is restored" simply do not appear any more.

When building a highly available Mailbox Server environment in a DAG, there's no need to build a fail-over cluster in advance, as additional Mailbox Servers can be added to the DAG on the fly. However, for the DAG to function properly, some fail-over clustering components are still used, but these are installed during DAG's configuration. All Management of the DAG and the database copies is performed via the Exchange Management Console or the Exchange Management Shell; the Windows Cluster Manager is no longer used.

Note

The Database Availability Group with Database Copies is the only high availability technology used in Exchange Server 2010. Older technologies like SCR, CCR and SCR are no longer available. The traditional Single Copy Cluster (SCC) with shared storage is also no longer supported.

Configuration of a Database Availability Group is no longer limited to a server holding just the Mailbox Server Role. It is possible to create a two-server situation with the Hub Transport, Client Access and Mailbox Server role on both servers, and then create a Database Availability Group and configure Database Copies. However, it isn't a High Availability configuration for the Client Access or Hub Transport servers unless you've put load balancers in front of them, since it's not possible to use the default Windows Network Load Balancing (NLB) in combination with the fail-over clustering components. Regardless, this is a great improvement for smaller deployments of Exchange Server 2010 where high availability is still required.

5.3.2.1 Active Manager

In Exchange Server 2007, Cluster Continuous Replication uses the cluster resource management model to install and manage the High Availability solution. Initially, the Windows cluster is built and then Exchange setup is run in clustered mode, registering the EXRES.DLL in the failover-cluster, and the Clustered Mailbox Server (CMS) was created. For a High Available Exchange Server 2007 environment it is *always* necessary to build a fail-over cluster in advance, even if it's just a one-node cluster!

The cluster components are now hidden in Exchange Server 2010, and a new component named the *Active Manager* has been introduced. The Active Manager replaces the resource model and fail-over management features offered in previous versions of Exchange Server.

The fail-over clustering components have not been completely removed, though, and some of them are actually still used. If you open the Fail-over Cluster Manager in Administrative Tools, you'll find the DAG, cluster networks, etc. *Do not* try to manage the DAG using the Failover Cluster Manager, as this is not supported. The only way to manage the DAG is using the Exchange Management Console or the Exchange Management Shell!

The Active Manager runs on all Mailbox Servers that are members of a DAG, and there are two roles; the Primary Active Manager (PAM) and the Standby Active Manager (SAM). The PAM is running on the Mailbox Server that also holds the cluster quorum, and this is the server that decides which databases are active and which databases are passive in a DAG. The SAM is responsible for determining server or database failures (the PAM does this on its own server for its own local databases) and, if detected, communicates with the PAM to initiate a failover.

The replication service monitors the health of the mounted databases in a DAG, and monitors the ESE engine for any I/O issues or failures. If anything goes wrong here, the replication service immediately contacts the Active Manager. In the case of a failover, the Active Manager determines which database should become the Active Copy of the database (depending on the fail-over order you've specified during configuration).

5.3.3 Configuring a Database Availability Group

To configure a Database Availability Group, at least two Exchange Server 2010 Mailbox Servers are required. Imagine a four server deployment, one Exchange Server 2010 Client Access Server, one Exchange Server 2010 Hub Transport Server and two Exchange Server 2010 Mailbox Servers (EXMBX01 and EXMBX11). All four servers are located in the same Active Directory site, and this site is also the Internet-facing Active Directory site.

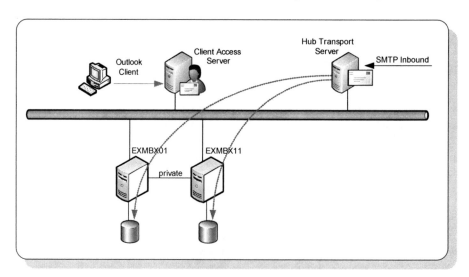

Figure 7: A four server Exchange 2010 deployment.

Let's assume that all four servers are fully operational and working fine. To create a Database Availability Group for the two Mailbox Servers, an additional private network is needed, which will be used for replication purposes.

To create a Database Availability Group follow these steps.

1.   Log on to an Exchange Server and open the Exchange Management Console.

2.   Expand the *Exchange On-Premises (SERVER)*, and then expand the Organization leaf.
     Click the Mailbox and then click the Database Availability Group tab. No items will be
     shown in the results pane.

3.   On the Mailbox Server, open the Exchange Management Shell and then enter the
     following command:

```
New-DatabaseAvailabilityGroup -Name DAG1
-DatabaseAvailabilityGroupIpAddresses 10.0.0.101
```

4.   A new Database Availability Group with the IP address of 10.0.0.101 will be created. Since
     the Database Availability Group is nothing more than a placeholder in Active Directory,
     it can be seen with ADSIEdit.

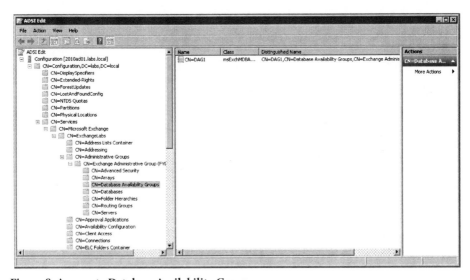

Figure 8: An empty Database Availability Group.

5.   To add the first Mailbox Server (EXMBX01) to the Database Availability Group, switch
     back to the Exchange Management Shell and enter the following command:

```
Add-DatabaseAvailabilityGroupServer -Identity DAG1 -MailboxServer
EXMBX01
```

6. The specified Mailbox Server will now be added to the Database Availability Group. Furthermore, a File Share Witness will be created on the Hub Transport Server. The File Share Witness, just like in an Exchange Server 2007 CCR environment, is needed to create a majority in the cluster when a server fails. The actual addition of the Mailbox Server and the creation of the File Share Witness can take up to 45 seconds.

7. When switching back to the Exchange Management Console you can now see the Database Availability Group (DAG1) in the console, as well as the EXMBX01 we just added.

8. Click the Database Management tab in the Exchange Management Console. You'll see the initial databases on the first and second Mailbox Servers. Also notice that there's one database copy available on each server. When you select the Public Folder Database in the Database Management tab, the Database Copies results pane is grayed-out. This is because Public Folder replication and Database Replication are not compatible.

9. To add the second Exchange Server 2010 Mailbox Server to the Database Availability Group, log on to the second server and open the Exchange Management Shell. Enter the following command:

```
Add-DatabaseAvailabilityGroupServer -Identity DAG1 -MailboxServer
EXMBX11
```

10. The second Mailbox Server will now be added to the Database Availability Group. As with adding the first Mailbox Server, this can take several seconds to finish.

Note

If the Windows Fail-over clustering components are not already installed on the Mailbox Server, they automatically will be. You can also manually install them in advance by opening a command prompt and execute the following command:

```
ServerManagerCmd.exe -i Failover-Clustering
```

Right, now we have created a Database Availability Group with two mailbox servers and we're ready to configure Database Copies. The Database Availability Group feature is very flexible. As I've explained, there's no need to configure a Windows Fail-over cluster in advance; you can add a Mailbox Server to the DAG whenever needed – even a year later – without a problem. Just install a Mailbox Server, install the Fail-over clustering bits, and add the server to the DAG. This is known as *Incremental Deployment*.

It is also possible to create site resilience using the Database Availability Group. Besides adding Mailbox Servers in the same Active Directory site (i.e. in the same datacenter), you can also add Mailbox Servers in another Active Directory site, such as in another datacenter. As long as the network connectivity is good enough to handle the replication in a timely manner, and as long as the Hub Transport and Client Access Servers have a reliable network connection to the other datacenter, you're ready to go.

If you want to add a Mailbox Server in another site to the DAG, a few configuration changes are needed. The IP Address of the DAG in the other site has to be added to the local DAG, and since this is not possible with the Exchange Management Console, the Exchange Management Shell has to be used. Enter the following command:

```
Set-DatabaseAvailabilityGroup -Identity DAG1
-DatabaseAvailabilityGroupIpAddresses 10.0.0.101,192.168.1.101
```

The first network in the DAG will be automatically created during the addition of the first Mailbox Server. Additional networks are not created automatically, so you have to add the subnet of the second site to the DAG manually:

```
New-DatabaseAvailabilityGroupNetwork -DatabaseAvailabilityGroup
DAG1
-Name DAGNetwork02 -Description "Second Site" -Subnets
192.168.1.0/24
-ReplicationEnabled:$True
```

Note

If there are Domain Controllers in the site you just added, you must wait for the replication to finish, or else force the replication to start. Otherwise the Domain Controllers in the second site may not have enough knowledge about the changes you want to make.

At this stage you can add a Mailbox Server in the second site to the DAG using the Exchange Management Console or the Exchange Management Shell:

```
Add-DatabaseAvailabilityGroupServer -Identity DAG1 -MailboxServer
EXMBX02
```

5.3.4 Managing database copies

A database copy is exactly what its name implies: a copy of an active database, but on another Exchange Server, in the same Database Availability Group. When initially configured, a copy of the database file is copied via the network to the other server and when finished, Exchange Server 2010 starts replication of the log files of this particular database over the network to the other server.

The relative location of the passive copy of the database is also identical to the location of the active copy. For example, an initial database on an Exchange Server 2010 Mailbox Server can be located in the directory "C:\Program Files\Microsoft\Exchange Server\V14\Mailbox\Mailbox Database 1444276156." If a database copy is enabled for this server, the same directory is created on the second server. The process of copying a database to a second location is known as *seeding*.

It is best practice to use separate disks for Exchange Databases, both from a performance perspective as well as a disaster recovery perspective. Although meant for earlier versions of Exchange Server, Microsoft Knowledge Base article 328794 explains more: HTTP://TINYURL. COM/SEPARATEDISKS.

After configuring "*Mailbox Database 1444276156*" to use the separate disk G:\ for storing its information, the database copy can be configured:

1. On the target server, i.e. the server that will hold the database copy, make sure there's an identical volume as on the source server. The target server in this example needs a separate G:\ disk as well.

2. Open the Exchange Management Console, expand the "*Microsoft Exchange On-Premises (EXMBX01)*", then expand the Organization Configuration container, and then click on the Mailbox node. Select the Database Management tab.

3. Select "*Mailbox Database 1444276156.*" In the lower part of the results pane there's one copy, the active copy, located on the first Exchange server EXMBX01. Right-click "*Mailbox Database 1444276156*" and select "*Add Mailbox Database Copy...*"

4. In the *Add Mailbox Database Copy* wizard, select "*Browse*" to select a Mailbox Server that will hold a copy of the database. The "*Activation Preference Number*" is the order in which Exchange will make a passive copy into an active copy when the preceding active copy fails. Of course, this number is only useful if multiple passive copies are configured (a complete rundown of the Activation Preference Number and what happens when a database becomes active is on the Microsoft TechNet website: HTTP://TINYURL.COM/ ACTIVEMANAGER). Click Add to continue.

5. The database file "*Mailbox Database 1444276156.edb*" will now be copied to the target server and the replication will be set up. Depending of the size of the Database file, this can take some time.

6. When the database is copied and the replication is activated, click Finish.

Once completed, log on to the target Exchange server and you'll notice that on this server (on the G:\ disk in this example) a "*Mailbox Database 1444276156*" directory has been created where the copy of the database is stored. You'll also see the log files that are replicated to this directory.

If a lot of databases are used on an Exchange Server, using mount points is a valid alternative. In a mount point scenario, all data disks are mounted to a directory on the server, for example F:\DB01, F:\DB02, F:\DB03, etc., using Server Manager.

In an Exchange Server 2007 CCR environment, the active server also ships log files to the passive server, which also loads the log files into its copy of the database. However, the passive server is *really* passive, and the service responsible for the database and the log files (store.exe) is not running. The only service that is running is the replication service. During a failover, the passive node has to start all Exchange services, and all databases need to be mounted before that can happen. In Exchange Server 2010 the store.exe service is already running and the databases are already mounted on all computers in a Database Availability Group, meaning a database failover is much faster, and the result is a much shorter overall failover time.

For maintenance purposes it is possible to move an active database copy from one Exchange Mailbox server to another:

1. Log on to an Exchange Server and open the Exchange Management Console.

2. Expand the *Exchange On-Premises (SERVER)*, and then expand the Organization leaf. Click the Mailbox and then click the Database Management tab.

3. All of the databases in your Exchange Server 2010 environment show up in the upper half of the results pane. Right-click the database you want to move (which is, of course, also a database that has multiple copies configured).

4. Select "*Move Active Mailbox Database*" from the context menu.

5. In the "*Move Active Mailbox Database*" wizard select *Browse* to select another server where you want the Active Copy to be moved to.

6. Click the *Move* button to move the Active Copy of the database to the server just selected.

5.3.5 Online Move-Mailbox

The online Move-Mailbox feature is new in Exchange Server 2010. In older versions of Exchange Server, the mailbox is taken offline when it is being moved from one server to another server, to prevent users from accessing any of their data, and queuing up any incoming messages . There are situations when a huge (5GB) mailbox has to be kept offline for more than an hour while the move takes place! None of these make for a particularly usable system.

With the new online Move-Mailbox functionality, now called New-MoveRequest, the time a mailbox is offline has been reduced to only seconds and, as such, the end-user experience has been *greatly* improved.

This is what happens during an online Move-Mailbox, when a mailbox is moved (see Figure 9) from one server (*EXBMX01*) to another server in the same organization (*EXMBX11*), for example:

1. On Mailbox Server EXMBX11, an empty copy of the user's mailbox is created, just like a "legacy" move-mailbox operation. But instead of taking the current mailbox offline (on EXMBX01), the original mailbox is kept online. This is still the primary mailbox for the client, and new messages still are delivered in this mailbox.

2. The contents of the "old" mailbox are copied over to the mailbox on server EXMBX11 and this mailbox is synchronized with the old mailbox.

3. As new items are delivered to the old mailbox, they are immediately copied over to the new mailbox.

4. When both mailboxes are in sync, the old mailbox is taken offline and the last messages are copied over to the new mailbox.

5. Active Directory is updated with the location of the new mailbox, and the mailbox is brought online again. The user may need to restart their Outlook client, but the Client Access Server should automatically detect that the mailbox has moved, and start using the new location. Either way, the user can continue working in just a matter of seconds.

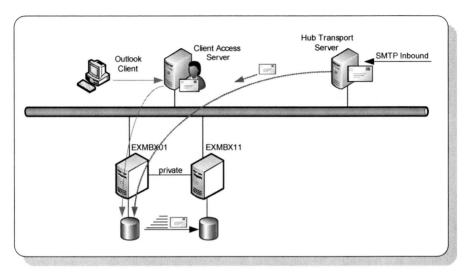

Figure 9: Online Move-Mailbox.

The online Move-Mailbox not only works between Exchange Server 2010 Mailbox Servers, but also when moving mailboxes from Exchange Server 2007 SP2 to Exchange Server 2010. Unfortunately, moving from Exchange Server 2010 to Exchange Server 2007 is still an offline move.

Likewise, moving mailboxes from Exchange Server 2003 to Exchange Server 2010 is always an offline move.

5.3.6 Backup and restore

Exchange Server 2010 only runs on Windows Server 2008 and Windows Server 2008 R2. This means that the (free) NTBackup utility in Windows Server 2003 cannot be used to back up Mailbox Databases on Exchange Server 2010. In any case, NTBackup was only capable of creating "streaming backups" of your Exchange data, not Volume Shadowcopy Service (VSS) backups of your Exchange database. Exchange Server 2010 contains a plug-in for the Windows Server Backup (WSB) to make it possible to create VSS backups of your Exchange Server 2010 databases.

5.3.6.1 VSS or snapshot backups

With Exchange Server 2010, Microsoft has finally moved away from the traditional online streaming backup to VSS (or "*snapshot*") backups. A snapshot is just an image of a database created at a particular point in time, which can be used to roll back the database in case of a disaster. The *Volume Shadow Copy Service*, in Windows Server 2003 and later, provides an infrastructure to create these point-in-time images, which are called *Shadow Copies*.

There are two kinds of Shadow Copies:

- **Clone** (Full Copy or Split Mirror) – a complete mirror is maintained until an application or administrator breaks the mirror. From this point on, the original and the clone are fully independent of each other, and the copy is effectively frozen in time.

- **Copy on Write** (Differential Copy) – a shadow copy is created as a differential rather than a full copy of the original data. Using Copy on Write, a shadow copy of the original data is made before it is overwritten. Effectively, the backup consists of the data in the shadow copy combined with the data on the original location, and both need to be available to reconstruct the original data.

The Volume Shadow Copy Infrastructure consists of the following components:

- **Requestor** – this is the software that invokes the VSS and creates, breaks or deletes the shadow copy. The Requestor is typically the backup application.

- **Writer** – a software part that is provided by an application vendor. In our case this is provided with the Microsoft Exchange Server. A writer is responsible for providing a consistent point-in-time image by freezing or quiescing the Exchange Server at the relevant moment. Please note that an Exchange writer is provided for Exchange Server 2003 and higher, right out of the box.

- **Provider** – a provider is the interface to the point-in-time image. This can either be on a storage array (hardware provider) or in the Operating System (software provider). Windows Server 2003 and above incorporate a software Provider with VSS functionality out of the box.

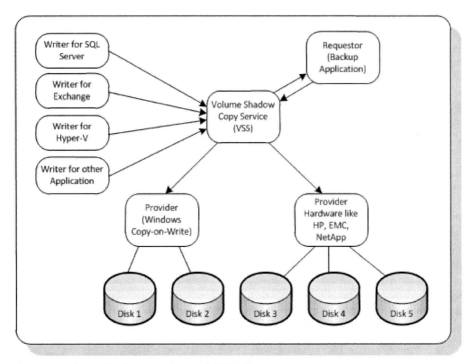

Figure 10: Volume Shadowcopy Server (VSS) Infrastructure.

The following steps occur when a VSS backup is performed:

1. The Requestor (i.e. the backup application) sends a command to the Volume Shadow Copy Service to create a shadow copy of the Storage Groups.

2. The VSS service sends a command to the Exchange writer to prepare for a snapshot backup.

3. The VSS service sends a command to the appropriate storage provider to create a shadow copy of the Exchange Storage Group. This storage provider can be a hardware storage provider or the default Windows storage provider.

4. The Exchange writer temporarily stops or quiesces the Storage Group and puts them in read-only mode. A log file roll-over is also performed to make sure that all data will be in the backup set. This will hold a couple of seconds for the snapshot to be created (in the next step). All write I/Os will be queued.

5. The shadow copy is now created.

6. The VSS service releases the Exchange server to resume ordinary operations and all queued write I/Os are completed.

7. The VSS service queries the Exchange writer to confirm that the write I/Os were successfully held during the shadow copy creation. If the writes were not successfully held it could mean a potentially inconsistent shadow copy, so the shadow copy is deleted and the requestor is notified. The requestor can retry the shadow copy process or fail the operation.

8. If successful, the requestor creates either a differential or a clone snapshot, and then verifies the integrity of the backup set (the clone copy). If the clone copy integrity is good, the requestor informs the Exchange Server that the backup was successful and that the log files can be purged. The backup is now complete.

Note

It is the responsibility of the backup application to perform a consistency check of the shadow copy. The Exchange writer does not perform this check.

Steps 1 through 7 usually take about 10 seconds, as this is the time needed to create the actual snapshot. This is not the time to create a backup, though. A backup application still has to create the backup on another disk or to tape, which can still take hours to complete depending on the size of the databases.

5.3.6.2 Backup with Windows Server Backup

Windows Server Backup is a feature in Windows 2008 (R2), and it can be installed using the Server Manager. Open the Server Manager, select Features, and then select the Windows Server Backup in the feature list to install it. When backing up your Exchange data using Windows Server Backup, at least one disk is needed to store the backups. This can be either a physical disk in the server or a disk on a storage device.

When starting Windows Server Backup there's no indication that it is Exchange Server 2010 aware; when the Exchange databases are located on drive G:\ and drive H:\, these drives have to be manually selected in Windows Server Backup. After selecting these disks, *another* disk needs to be selected to store the actual backup. This can be any disk, except the ones that are being backed up or the system disk (i.e. the C:\ drive). When the backup is running, you'll notice that Windows Server Backup checks the Exchange database for consistency.

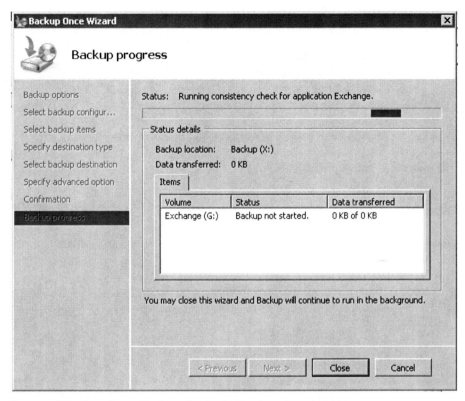

Figure 11: Windows Server Backup checks the database for consistency.

When Windows Server Backup has finished backing up the Exchange database, the header of the database is updated with relevant backup information. The status of the database can be examined using ESEUTIL /MH:

```
G:\mailbox database 0242942819>eseutil /mh  "mailbox database
0242942819.edb"

Extensible Storage Engine Utilities for Microsoft(R) Exchange
Server
Version 14.00
Copyright (C) Microsoft Corporation. All Rights Reserved.

Initiating FILE DUMP mode...
        Database: mailbox database 0242942819.edb

Previous Full Backup:
        Log Gen: 4-5 (0x4-0x5) - OSSnapshot
```

```
            Mark: (0x6,8,16)
            Mark: 08/08/2009 11:39:06

    Previous Incremental Backup:
          Log Gen: 0-0 (0x0-0x0)
            Mark: (0x0,0,0)
            Mark: 00/00/1900 00:00:00

    Operation completed successfully in 0.31 seconds.

    G:\mailbox database 0242942819>
```

[Edited for readability]

Windows Server Backup also logs all activities in the Eventlog. When checking the Eventviewer you'll see the ESE and MSExhangeIS events, like:

```
    Log Name:       Application
    Source:         ESE
    Date:           8-8-2009 11:39:05
    Event ID:       2005
    Task Category: ShadowCopy
    Level:          Information
    Keywords:       Classic
    User:           N/A
    Computer:       EXMBX12.labs.local
    Description:
    Information Store (2444) Shadow copy instance 1 starting. This
    will be a Full shadow copy.

    For more information, click http://www.microsoft.com/
    contentredirect.asp.
```

And

```
    Log Name:       Application
    Source:         MSExchangeIS
    Date:           8-8-2009 11:39:05
    Event ID:       9811
    Task Category: Exchange VSS Writer
    Level:          Information
    Keywords:       Classic
```

```
User:           N/A
Computer:       EXMBX12.labs.local
Description:
Exchange VSS Writer (instance 1) has successfully prepared the
database engine for a full or copy backup of database 'mailbox
database 0242942819'.
```

When the backup has successfully finished, the log files will be purged as well. Which log files are purged will depend on how busy the server is during backup (lots of new messages, moving mailbox, etc.) and the checkpoint depth. Purging the log files is logged in the Eventlog as well:

```
Log Name:       Application
Source:         ESE
Date:           8-8-2009 11:39:19
Event ID:       224
Task Category: ShadowCopy
Level:          Information
Keywords:       Classic
User:           N/A
Computer:       EXMBX12.labs.local
Description:
Information Store (2444) mailbox database 0242942819: Deleting
log files G:\mailbox database 0242942819\E0000000001.log to
G:\mailbox database 0242942819\E0000000003.log.
```

Note

Windows Server Backup is only capable of creating a full backup or a copy backup. Incremental or differential backups are not supported.

5.3.6.3 Windows Server Backup and database replication

Windows Server Backup can also create backups of databases that are in a Database Administration Group (DAG), although a limitation of WSB is that it can only create a backup of an active copy of the database. If you create a backup of an active copy, the backup will succeed, but when the active copy moves to another server and the local database becomes passive, the backup will now fail!

The process of creating backups is identical as in earlier paragraphs, except for the truncation of log files. Log files are only truncated if all log files are replicated and relayed to other database copies. Only then will the log files on the active copy be truncated. This can take some time, which is no reason for worry. It is also logged in the Eventlog:

```
Log Name:        Application
Source:          MSExchangeIS
Date:            8-8-2009 11:54:16
Event ID:        9827
Task Category:   Exchange VSS Writer
Level:           Information
Keywords:        Classic
User:            N/A
Computer:        EXMBX01.labs.local
Description:
Exchange VSS Writer (instance 725e6ff5-7fd0-4c52-9bf1-
f62fafc425ea:5) has successfully completed the full or
incremental backup of replicated database 'Mailbox Database
1444276156'. The log files will be truncated after they have been
replayed.
```

5.4 High Availability on other server roles

For a complete Highly Available Exchange Server 2010 environment, not only do the Mailbox Servers need to be configured as such, but also the Hub Transport Servers, Client Access Servers and, if used, the Edge Transport Servers. The High Availability configurations for these other server roles are quite different from the Mailbox server role, but very similar to their Exchange Server 2007 configurations (which is why I'm not spending much time on them).

5.4.1 Hub Transport Servers

For redundancy of transport at least two Hub Transport Servers are needed. When creating a Send Connector, you can define the Source Server that sends out the messages over this connector and, for redundancy, you can add a second Hub Transport Server as a source server.

1. Log on to an Exchange Server and open the Exchange Management Console.

2. Expand the *Exchange On-Premises (SERVER)*, and then expand the Organization leaf. Click the Hub Transport leaf and select the Send Connectors tab.

3. Right-click the *Send Connector* that needs to be changed and select *Properties*.

4. In the properties of the Send Connector select the *Source Server* tab.

5. Click the Add button to add a second Hub Transport Server to the Send Connector.

6. After selecting the second server, click OK twice.

The Hub Transport Server will now have a redundant path, and will automatically load balance outbound messages over both source servers. A Round Robin mechanism is used for load balancing outbound SMTP traffic on both Hub Transport servers.

For inbound messaging, a load balancing solution needs to be manually implemented. This can be an ISA Server 2006 or any other hardware device that's capable of load balancing SMTP traffic. You can also use Windows Server 2008 Network Load Balancing, as this is an out-of-the-box Microsoft solution. Using NLB, a load balancing solution can be built running on Windows which then keeps track of all the incoming connections and automatically load balances the requests between the Hub Transport Servers. This is a fully supported solution (since Exchange Server 2007 SP1). The last option is to use DNS Round Robin to load balance incoming traffic.

Note

NLB is only supported for inbound SMTP connections, not for outbound SMTP connections, and cannot be installed on any server hosting a DAG. A server hosting a DAG must have Windows Fail-over Clustering in operation, and NLB cannot coexist with WFP.

5.4.2 Client Access Servers

For redundancy on the Client Access Server layer at least two servers need to be implemented, which should be load balanced on the *protocol* layer. The load balancing solution can either be a Microsoft ISA Server 2006 solution or a hardware-based load balancing solution. As with the Hub Transport Server, NLB can also be used for load balancing the connections on the Client Access Server (unless it's hosting a DAG).

5.4.3 Edge Transport Servers

When using an Edge Transport solution in the Demilitarized Zone (DMZ) of your network, at least two Edge Transport Servers need to be implemented. Bear in mind that all Edge Transport Servers have their own instance of the Active Directory Lightweight Directory Service (AD LDS, previously known as ADAM, Active Directory Application Mode), and all Edge Transport Servers have their own subscription to the Hub Transport Servers in the company network.

When multiple Edge Transport Servers are connected to the same site, they are all automatically added as source servers to the inbound Send Connector. Load balancing takes place across these Edge Transport Servers in the same way that load balancing takes place on the Hub Transport Servers.

5.5 Summary

With the new Database Availability Group functionality in Exchange Server 2010, you now have the ability to create high availability solutions on the Mailbox Server level, and this functionality replaces the Continuous Cluster Replication (CCR) and Stand-by Continuous Cluster Replication (SCR) in Exchange 2007. To be honest, the Database Availability Group is what CCR/SCR should have been. It is flexible, powerful and less complex than the CCR/SCR solution, and it combines the best of both worlds. I really recommend that everybody start looking at the Database Availability Group and, whenever possible, implement it.

The High Availability Solutions on the Hub Transport Server role and Client Access Server role are implemented using protocol load balancing. This can be achieved using a hardware load balancer, Windows Network Load Balancing (NLB) or by using DNS Round Robin. This hasn't changed much though compared to Exchange Server 2007, so I've only touched upon it lightly. Having read this chapter you should now be able to ensure your Exchange Server Organization is always up and running when needed. Of course, as this is a just a practical guide to get you started, there's much more to learn to make your Exchange environment disaster-proof!

Index

Symbols

SQL Tools
from **Red Gate Software**

Exchange Server Archiver

Email archiving software for Exchange

↗ Email archiving for Exchange Server

↗ Reduce size of information store – no more PSTs/mailbox quotas

↗ Archive only the mailboxes you want to

↗ Exchange, Outlook, and OWA 2003 and 2007 supported

↗ Transparent end-user experience – message preview, instant retrieval, and integrated search

"Exchange Server Archiver is almost 100% invisible to Outlook end-users. The tool is simple to install and manage. This combined with the ability to set up different rules depending on user mailbox, makes the system easy to configure for all types of situations. I'd recommend this product to anyone who needs to archive exchange email."

Matthew Studer Riverside Radiology Associates

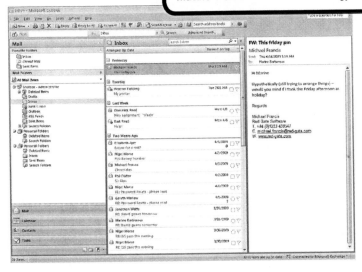

SQL Compare Pro $595

Compare and synchronize SQL Server database schemas

- ↗ Automate database comparisons, and synchronize your databases
- ↗ Simple, easy to use, 100% accurate
- ↗ Save hours of tedious work, and eliminate manual scripting errors
- ↗ Work with live databases, snapshots, script files or backups

"SQL Compare and SQL Data Compare are the best purchases we've made in the .NET/SQL environment. They've saved us hours of development time and the fast, easy-to-use database comparison gives us maximum confidence that our migration scripts are correct. We rely on these products for every deployment."

Paul Tebbutt Technical Lead, Universal Music Group

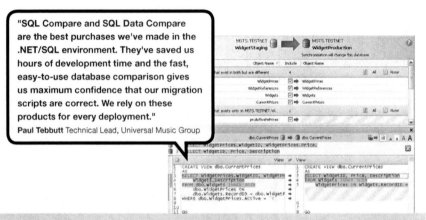

SQL Data Compare Pro $595

Compare and synchronize SQL Server database contents

- ↗ Compare your database contents
- ↗ Automatically synchronize your data
- ↗ Row-level data restore
- ↗ Compare to scripts, backups or live databases

"We use SQL Data Compare daily and it has become an indispensible part of delivering our service to our customers. It has also streamlined our daily update process and cut back literally a good solid hour per day."

George Pantela GPAnalysis.com

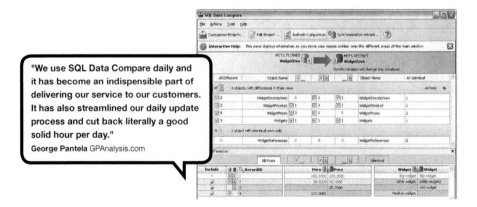

SQL Backup Pro $795

Compress, encrypt and monitor SQL Server backups

↗ Compress database backups by up to 95% for faster backups and restores

↗ Protect your data with up to 256-bit AES encryption

↗ Strengthen your backups with network resilience to enable the fault-tolerant transfer of backups across flaky networks

↗ Save time and space with the SQL Object Level Recovery Pro™ feature, so you can recover individual database objects instead of full database backups

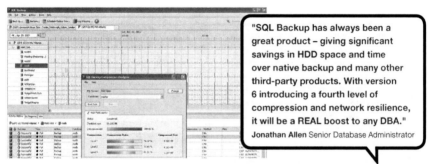

"SQL Backup has always been a great product – giving significant savings in HDD space and time over native backup and many other third-party products. With version 6 introducing a fourth level of compression and network resilience, it will be a REAL boost to any DBA."

Jonathan Allen Senior Database Administrator

Want to find out more?

Phone 1 866 997 0380 toll free or email backup.info@red-gate.com

SQL Response $495

Monitors SQL Servers, with alerts and diagnostic data

↗ Intuitive interface to enable easy SQL Server monitoring, configuration and analysis.

↗ Email alerts as soon as problems arise

↗ Investigate long-running queries, SQL deadlocks, blocked processes and more to resolve problems sooner

↗ Low-impact monitoring and no installation of components on your SQL Servers.

↗ Fast, simple installation and administration

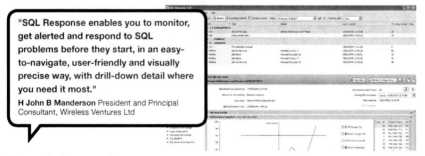

"SQL Response enables you to monitor, get alerted and respond to SQL problems before they start, in an easy-to-navigate, user-friendly and visually precise way, with drill-down detail where you need it most."

H John B Manderson President and Principal Consultant, Wireless Ventures Ltd

Want to find out more?

Phone 1 866 997 0380 toll free or email backup.info@red-gate.com

SQL Prompt Pro $295

The fastest way to work with SQL.

- ↗ Code-completion for SQL Server, including suggestions for complete join conditions
- ↗ Automated SQL reformatting with extensive flexibility to match your preferred style
- ↗ Rapid access to your database schema information through schema panes and tooltips
- ↗ Snippets let you insert common SQL fragments with just a few keystrokes

"With over 2000 objects in one database alone, SQL Prompt is a lifesaver! Sure, with a few mouse clicks I can get to the column or stored procedure name I am looking for but with SQL Prompt it is always right in front of me. SQL Prompt is easy to install, fast and easy to use. I hate to think of working without it!"

Michael Weiss LTCPCMS, Inc

SQL Data Generator $295

Test data generator for SQL Server databases

- ↗ Data generation in one click
- ↗ Realistic data based on column and table name
- ↗ Data can be customized if desired
- ↗ Eliminates hours of tedious work

"Red Gate's SQL Data Generator has overnight become the principal tool we use for loading test data to run our performance and load tests."

Grant Fritchey Principal DBA, FM Global

🖻 Preview of data to be generated (first 100 lines)

TitleOfCourtesy *Title*	BirthDate *datetime*	HireDate *datetime*	Address *Address Line (Stree*	City *US City*	Region *Region*	PostalCode *ZIP Code*	Country *Country*	HomeP *Phone*
Dr	23/08/1963 04:0...	25/04/1992 20:0...	37 Fabien St.	Richmond	IA-CT	58907	Gibraltar	12353:
Miss	10/01/1960 23:2...	16/02/1976 11:2...	850 White Nobel...	NULL	NV-EW	39330	Tajikistan	69862:
Mr	27/07/1970 13:5...	03/12/1953 15:3...	45 Green Milton...	New York	TN-OH	60387	Liberia	529-89
Mr	27/01/2002 04:3...	24/07/1958 00:5...	48 Milton Boulev...	Sacramento	NM-JR	13294	Côte d'Ivoire	984-11
Mr	31/05/1994 04:1...	12/01/1964 04:4...	592 Rocky Cowl...	Santa Ana	MI-UU	NULL	Jersey	417-47
Mrs	17/11/1975 10:1...	27/10/1968 18:5...	69 Clarendon Pa...	San Jose	IL-TC	41768	New Caledonia	11305(
Dr.	16/05/1974 06:1...	25/11/1998 14:5...	207 Fabien Blvd.	Houston	AL-GE	04937	Belgium	89687{
Dr	27/12/1999 19:4...	03/05/1972 13:1...	53 Rocky Oak R...	Baton Rouge	MA-RT	65364	Swaziland	076-87
Dr	14/10/1971 03:1...	28/06/1978 10:0...	260 East Rocky...	Charlotte	AL-AR	97727	Benin	54684!
Mr	09/11/1981 13:2...	26/12/2001 15:0...	476 North Fabie...	Akron	MA-IU	94269	Palau	87561:
Dr	28/06/1987 01:3...	30/10/1972 00:0...	48 South Hague...	Norfolk	VT-UV	66385	American Samoa	89085(
Mr	20/10/1962 04:4...	07/09/2005 17:1...	939 Fabien Park...	Grand Rapids	HI-YT	86033	Swaziland	58415(
Mr	25/01/2001 08:0...	18/08/1983 12:0...	348 North Green...	Wichita	FL-IV	32302	Zambia	124-42
Mr	05/01/1955 10:0...	12/08/1983 22:5...	32 Cowley Boule...	Spokane	WV-OI	45980	Chile	457-22

SQL Toolbelt™ $1,995

The essential SQL Server tools for database professionals.

You can buy our acclaimed SQL Server tools individually or bundled. Our most popular deal is the SQL Toolbelt: all thirteen of our SQL Server tools in a single installer, with **a combined value of $5,635 but an actual price of $1,995**, a saving of 65%.

*Fully compatible with SQL Server 2000, 2005 and **2008**!*

SQL Doc

Generate documentation for your SQL Server databases

↗ Produce clear and legible HTML or MS Word reports for multiple databases
↗ Documentation is stored as part of the database
↗ Output completed documentation to a range of different formats

$295

SQL Dependency Tracker

The graphical tool for tracking database and cross-server dependencies

↗ Visually track database object dependencies
↗ Discover all cross-database and cross-server object relationships
↗ Analyze potential impact of database schema changes
↗ Rapidly document database dependencies for reports, version control, and database change planning

$295

SQL Packager

Compress and package your databases for easy installations and upgrades

↗ Script your entire database accurately and quickly
↗ Move your database from A to B
↗ Compress your database as an exe file, or launch as a Visual Studio project
↗ Simplify database deployments and installations

$295

SQL Multi Script

Single-click script execution on multiple SQL Servers

↗ Cut out repetitive administration by deploying multiple scripts on multiple servers with just one click
↗ Return easy-to-read, aggregated results from your queries to export either as a csv or .txt file
↗ Edit queries fast with an intuitive interface, including colored syntax highlighting, Find and Replace, and split-screen editing

$195

SQL Comparison SDK

Automate database comparisons and synchronizations

↗ Full API access to Red Gate comparison tools
↗ Incorporate comparison and synchronization functionality into your applications
↗ Schedule any of the tasks you require from the SQL Comparison Bundle

$695

SQL Refactor

Refactor and format your SQL code

Twelve tools to help update and maintain databases quickly and reliably, including:

↗ Rename object and update all references
↗ Expand column wildcards, qualify object names, and uppercase keywords
↗ Summarize script
↗ Encapsulate code as stored procedure

$295

Confessions of an IT Manager
Phil Factor

The software industry is, just occasionally, more absurd than one would dare to imagine. Having spent most of his working life in its clutches, Phil Factor has pretty much "seen it all" and what's more he's prepared to tell what he knows. The second edition of Phil's "Confessions of an IT Manager" contains Phil's full repertoire of tales of institutional mayhem and software projects gone awry.

ISBN: 978-1-906434-19-9
Published: May 2009 (2nd Edition)

How to Become an Exceptional DBA
Brad McGehee

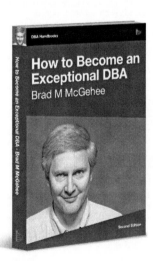

A career guide that will show you, step-by-step, exactly what you can do to differentiate yourself from the crowd so that you can be an Exceptional DBA. While Brad focuses on how to become an Exceptional SQL Server DBA, the advice in this book applies to any DBA, no matter what database software they use. If you are considering becoming a DBA, or are a DBA and want to be more than an average DBA, this is the book to get you started.

ISBN: 978-1-906434-23-6
Published: July 2009 (2nd Edition)

Protecting SQL Server Data
John Magnabosco

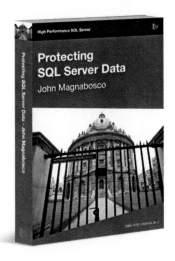

Protecting SQL Server Data holds the key to "encryption without fear." Data security expert, John Magnabosco sweeps away some of the misconceptions surrounding SQL Server's encryption technologies, and demonstrates that, when properly planned and implemented, they are an essential tool in the DBA's fight to safeguard sensitive data.

ISBN: 978-1-906434-27-4
Published: September 2009

Coming Soon: Brad's Sure Guide to SQL Server Maintenence Plans
Brad McGehee

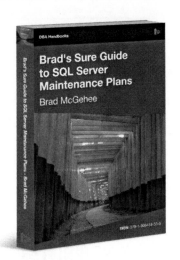

Brad's Sure Guide to Maintenance Plans shows you how to use the Maintenance Plan Wizard and Designer to configure and schedule eleven core database maintenance tasks, ranging from integrity checks, to database backups, to index reorganizations and rebuilds.

ISBN: 78-1-906434-34-2
Published: December 2009

Lightning Source UK Ltd.
Milton Keynes UK
16 April 2010

152899UK00001B/67/P